W9-BOB-466

Feel Better
Fast

Also by Dr. Charles Foster

What Do I Do Now?
Dr. Foster's 30 Laws of Great Decision Making

Truth Without Fear:
How to Communicate Difficult News in Tough Situations

Parent/Teen Breakthrough:
The Relationship Approach (with Mira Kishenbaum)

Feel Better
Fast

Overcoming the
Emotional Fallout
of Your Illness or Injury

Charles Foster, Ph.D.
Foreword by Mira Kirshenbaum

M. Evans and Company, Inc.
New York

M. Evans and Company, Inc.
216 East 49th Street
New York, New York 10017

www.mevans.com

Contents

To my parents

Welcome to the Medicine of the Future

by Mira Kirshenbaum
Author of *The Emotional Energy Factor*

Something absolutely essential has been missing in even the best health-care today: an understanding of the role emotions and psychology play when something goes wrong with the body. It's true that the best medical care tries to integrate Western and alternative approaches in an attempt to treat the body as a whole. But until now this integrative approach hasn't gone far enough.

It's time we took the final step in our understanding of where cure really comes from. It's time we took the word "holistic" to the highest level. It's no longer enough to look at the body as a whole. We need to look at the person as a whole. And so I advocate the ultimate in holistic medicine—*personal medicine*—which is the approach pioneered by Dr. Charles Foster in *Feel Better Fast*.

Personal medicine helps us see that it's not only our body that gets sick or injured. It's *we* who get sick or injured, you and I, the whole individual person. Of course our body is involved! But so are our feelings, our whole psychological selves. And it's only through understanding and addressing your emotions that you're able to integrate who you are as a person—your gender, ethnicity, personal history, everything that's vital to your sense of self—into your medical picture.

When emotions are left out, you're not dealing with everything necessary for a full and rapid recovery. You're only focusing on half the person. The medical establishment is just beginning to catch on to the fact that when you include the emotions in treatment, recoveries happen that once seemed impossible or infinitely delayed.

If you ask, "Are there currently any health issues with you or someone in your immediate family?" about 85 percent of people say *yes*. The emotional fallout from illness or injury doesn't stop with the people directly affected. It includes their spouses, parents, children, and friends. When you address this emotional fallout, a lot of people benefit.

I've had direct experience with the power of personal medicine. Several years ago, when I had to deal with a serious medical condition of my own, I had the chance to be one of the guinea pigs for the information in this book. By dealing with the emotions that came from what I was going through physically, it was astounding how well I felt in spite of my illness and how speedily I recovered. The help explained here has made all the difference for me, and I'm sure Dr. Foster has the right prescriptions for you, too.

Welcome to the Medicine of the Future

Feel Better Fast is personal medicine in action. This is the only book I know that shows you how to identify and neutralize all the emotional and psychological factors responsible for feeling lousy. Then Dr. Foster shows you exactly how to get back to feeling like yourself again.

Acknowledgments

This book would not have existed without the wholehearted participation of people I now consider my family. It's a darned big family—countless men and women of all ages and backgrounds—and I thank God for them. They are family not by blood but because they've shared their lives with me and because, on the deepest level, we have the same dreams and hold similar values: we all believe that the highest quality health-care is a right for everyone. And we believe that top-quality health-care must address the whole person—not just our bodies but all of our feelings and needs.

I call them my family even though there are some I've never met face to face. But they all shared with me their stories of how they dealt with some illness or injury. How they were frustrated by the many emotional issues that were coming up for them. And how those issues seemed to make it hard for them to get better as fast and as fully as possible. The stories of their frustrations and of the amazing solutions they discovered form the fabric of this book. I am eternally grateful to them all.

In these pages I am sometimes critical of health-care providers for not being sensitive to patients' emotional and psychological issues. This insensitivity makes the people they are treating want to say to them, "But I'm not a patient, I'm a person!" I will not back down from my assertion that far too many doctors have a lot to learn about treating the whole person. But I do realize that this is only a generality. I'd be remiss if I didn't also acknowledge the many wonderful doctors, nurses, and other health-care providers who have shared with me their dream of one day treating each patient as a whole person, and who are doing the best they can right now to make this happen. My own doctor, Carolyn Hope Kreinsen, M.D., exemplifies this still all-too-rare approach. People like Dr. Kreinsen are the real heroes of medicine today, and there will soon be many more like them.

I'm very grateful to my marvelous editor, PJ Dempsey. She has worked above and beyond the call of duty to make sure this book serves the reader. She is responsible for much of its strength. Whatever weaknesses there are, I assure you, are solely mine. Much gratitude also to the wonderful Dina Jordan, my publicist, for her brilliant efforts at bringing this book to people's attention. Much thanks, also, to Matt Harper for being so helpful.

You hear about those mythical agents who believe in their authors, stick with them, and make good things happen. They're not all mythical. Carol Mann is quite real, and

I'm very grateful to her for all she has done for me.

So many individuals have advised and inspired me in the course of writing this book that I couldn't possibly name them all. And if I tried I know I'd end up feeling badly because I'd left some people out. These people include colleagues, patients of mine, friends, family, and members of my church. You know who you are and you have my deepest gratitude.

To My Readers

'm sure you're already getting help for whatever's wrong with your body. But you're still not feeling as good as you'd like. If so, I have good news for you. If you address the emotional issues that accompany your physical problems, you will recover more quickly and completely than you thought possible.

If you're willing to look at the emotions that accompany your injury or illness, you have everything you need to prevent negative emotions from hindering your full recovery. *Feel Better Fast* will show you what to do.

This book is not just for people with health problems. The information here is also valuable for spouses, friends, family members, and healthcare providers. If you're dealing with someone who's sick or injured, you can use the material here to make suggestions that will help that person feel much better emotionally and much better overall.

Feel Better Fast

We all know that some diseases are contagious. Shouldn't health be contagious, too? Shouldn't it be possible to pass on ways of feeling better? This book is my attempt to pass on to you a massive dose of good health. It's based in part on what I've learned from people with medical problems like yours. I hope you'll take everything that benefits you here and pass it on to others.

Please visit me at www.DrCharlesFoster.com and let me know what in this book has helped you most. I'm always trying to learn more about what works best, so I can use it to help more people.

Dr. Charles Foster

1

The Missing Ingredient in Your Full Recovery

t happens to almost everyone—you get an illness or injury that's serious enough to throw you for a loop emotionally.

It could be anything. You get hurt in an accident, and it bums you out to look down the long road you face before you'll fully mend. Or you get sick and you're anxious because you're not sure what's really wrong with you or whether you'll ever fully recover. Or you're flat on your back in pain, and you're fed up with the way you've been feeling, with the people who are supposed to be helping you but aren't, with everything. Or you're not all that sick,

19

but your life is very complicated and this couldn't be coming at a worse time, so it leaves you feeling overwhelmed.

The emotional fallout from illness or injury consists of all the powerful negative emotional states people experience when something goes wrong with their bodies. You need to overcome this emotional fallout, because if you don't, it will get in the way of your achieving the fullest, fastest recovery. And to do this you need the kind of help you'll find in these pages.

It's not been appreciated until recently how much your feeling lousy comes from factors that go way beyond your physical symptoms. I know they can be pretty bad sometimes, but when something goes wrong with your body, you also pay a big price emotionally. After you say ouch, after you let out a couple of groans, some very strong emotions come flooding in.

Most doctors only treat your body. This is not enough. As one woman put it, "I want to be treated as a person. It's not just about my body. I've got feelings too." So it's no surprise that even though you've done what your doctor has told you, you still feel lousy.

Joe. A regular guy, married with two young kids, Joe, 36, works for a large electronics concern. In his job he visits companies and talks to people about their problems and how his firm's products can solve them.

One day a guy ran a red light and slammed into the right side of Joe's car. They say breaking up is hard to do— Joe got broken up in many places, and it was hard indeed.

So there's Joe, in a hospital bed, in pain, getting constantly poked and prodded, and he tells himself he needs to have a positive attitude. "I'm going to fight this, and I'm going to beat it," he says. And that's a great attitude to have. But when you're in a situation like Joe's, mere attitude is like a very small boat on a very stormy sea—better than nothing but too easily swept away by the currents. You'd sure like something sturdier.

His life was never in danger, but from the beginning all the doctor could say was that he'd "probably be mostly okay, but full recovery would take a long time." "*Probably* be *mostly* okay"? For Joe this opened up a nightmare. Translation: "quite possibly be significantly *not* okay." And into that nightmare walked visions of having to spend his life in a wheelchair, or always limping, or never being able to throw a ball or hold his child. And he had visions of pain that would never go away.

Right then the pain itself was pretty bad. Joe was on painkillers. But what if he became addicted to them? What if he couldn't handle the pain?

And what about work? Would he be able to go back to his old job?

And what about his wife? She was great throughout the ordeal. But what if Joe was, as he put it, "never completely, you know, a man again" after this?

All this was just one strand in the emotional crown of thorns that came to Joe along with his injuries.

There was also—and this really surprised Joe—a lot of anger. He was angry with himself. Yeah, he'd had a green light, but obviously there are crazy drivers out there, so he should have looked. If he'd just been a little more careful. . . . And he was angry with his doctors. This kind of upset him, because he knew they were good doctors doing their best. Still, sometimes they were maddeningly vague. Sometimes they just didn't seem to know what they were doing. Sometimes they were brusque, and Joe found himself wanting them to be much nicer to him.

He felt so vulnerable. And that led to sadness. Joe wasn't a guy who was given to bouts of depression. But when the sadness came upon him, Joe felt he wanted to curl up in a ball and never move again. A phrase kept going through his head: "My life is over." And then he'd start thinking about what a burden he was to his family, and he'd get even more depressed.

You see the picture. Problems with your body. Problems with your emotions. All tied up in one fat package. And yet we now have new understanding that shows how Joe could feel better, function better, and recover faster than he ever imagined possible.

Don't make the mistake of saying, yeah, but Joe was in pretty bad shape physically. This applies to all of us. Take Emily, for example.

Emily. She is a healthy young woman of 29. But Emily gets migraines every month or two, bad ones that knock her into bed for a couple of days. Fear is a big part of her condition. Of course there's always the fear that something will trigger a migraine. When she goes to bed, she can never count on being migraine-free when she wakes up. Emily is single, and it's hard for her to escape the fear that she'll never find a man who can deal with her frequent migraines.

And she always feels an undercurrent of anger towards her friends. They're great, but they just don't understand what she goes through. Emily feels very much alone.

Then Emily has to deal with other feelings that resist easy labels. What do you call the emotions she feels toward her doctor? She doesn't really like him but hates herself for feeling so dependent, because she's afraid that she won't find anyone better—plus she's sad because he's all she's got. And there's that emotionally charged confusion she feels when she talks with her doctor about getting a new medication, or pursuing yet one more form of alternative medicine. He usually resists her suggestions, and Emily can't tell if he's closed minded or if her suggestions really are stupid. All Emily knows is that she feels badly about feeling badly.

Beethoven. Finally let's look at a guy you're probably acquainted with—Beethoven. Most people know three things about him. Beethoven was a great composer. He went deaf. He was a grouchy oddball. The first two are true. The third is not really the whole story.

Going deaf almost brought Beethoven to a complete emotional breakdown. Even after he found ways to cope, not being able to carry on a normal conversation with people still made him grumpy. Even worse, though, were a series of stomach problems and other chronic conditions that often put him in an angry, despairing mood. And yet, deep down, Beethoven was a sunny, hearty, playful person. You'd have liked him as a buddy or a brother. Sadly, his good nature for most of his life was damaged by his emotional reactions to his many illnesses.

Joe, Emily, and Beethoven are no different from the rest of us. Everyone goes through similar emotions when something goes wrong with their body. Take me: if I just get the flu, as the days drag by I start feeling blue. I'm mad at myself for getting sick and mad at my wife for not taking perfect care of me. And I get scared—what if this turns into pneumonia, or it's really cancer?

Of course, the emotional issues you have to deal with are all highly specific to you and the details of your situation. If you work in an office, a leg injury might not make you afraid of losing your livelihood. But if you're a construction worker, the same injury has a tremendous emotional charge because there's a real possibility of your never being able to work at your occupation again. One way or another, painful emotions are *always* there, and if you want to help yourself, you have to deal with them.

YOUR RISK OF EMOTIONAL FALLOUT

Here's how to assess your risk of emotional fallout when something goes wrong with your body. Answer the following four questions:

Is your illness or injury striking you with a particular intensity? Intensity has to do with how strongly you're affected physically. Most of us get headaches or backaches from time to time, and we take some over-the-counter painkiller and carry on even if we still feel discomfort. But if the pain is so bad that we can't get out of bed, or can't even think straight, that's when dark emotions start crowding in. Other intense physical effects range from sleeplessness to feeling in a fog, from tremors to weakness—anything that significantly impairs the way you feel.

Are you afraid your illness or injury might last indefinitely? This has to do with your having a problem that just doesn't go away, turning into something *chronic*. We've all had coughs. But if the coughing lasts for weeks, the emotional frustration and discouragement build up. It's the same with hurting your leg. Walking around with a limp for a little while is not that big a deal. Having to walk around with a big limp for the rest of your life can have significant emotional fallout.

Is the quality of your life at risk because of your illness or injury? This gets at the idea of the gravity of your condition. Many of us have had the experience of feeling a lump on our body and immediately thinking *Cancer!* Obviously the prospect of death makes any illness or injury very grave and fraught with emotional fallout. But the prospect of death isn't the only thing that makes physical problems grave. There's disability. Disfigurement. Disruption. Discomfort. Any potential loss raises the stakes emotionally.

Are you feeling some uncertainty? Uncertainty accelerates emotional fallout. If you're feeling rotten and go to a doctor, a clear diagnosis usually makes you feel better. At least you know what the problem is. But anyone who's lived for months not knowing what's exactly wrong with him will fall prey to anxiety and frustration. There can also be uncertainty about when you'll get better, about what the best treatment is, and about the extent of your recovery. The greater the uncertainty, the greater the emotional fallout.

If you answered with a clear yes *to even one of these four questions, then you're at risk of significant emotional fallout from your illness or injury. The more questions you said* yes *to, the greater your risk.*

You must deal with this emotional fallout. It can affect your performance on the job and maybe damage your career. It can add strains that cause your relationship to unravel. It can damage the whole quality of your life.

MY STORY

I know firsthand about how we get hit emotionally when something goes wrong with our bodies. When I was in my late thirties, I had a heart attack. (I've been fine for a number of years now, thank God.) Surprisingly, the physical aspects of what happened to me were not so bad. Yes, I had chest pains, but they were no worse than a bad stomach ache. The tests I had to undergo were no more harrowing than a tough uphill run.

The emotional part of being a patient was far worse. For a long time I was afraid I could die at any moment. I was uneasy because I was never sure that I was getting the best treatment. I feared for my future—would I die young? Would I be able to work? Would I return to normal functioning? I had to deal with the fact that my wife started acting differently towards me. She was afraid, for example, that I'd drop dead during sex. Heart attacks are not an aphrodisiac!

What I didn't know at that time was how much everyone else with an injury or illness was dealing with emotional as well as physical burdens. But my cardiologist said something very wise: "It's important that you don't become a heart patient." But I *was* a heart patient! Yet he was right. Something was happening to my body, but the most important thing was that I minimize the emotional damage. Heart sick, okay—they were treating that. Mind sick, not okay—*not necessary, possibly very dangerous*.

So I let my body heal itself and I focused my energy on dealing with my troubled emotions. As I went for follow-up visits, my cardiologist kept commenting on what a strong, rapid recovery I was making.

HOW I CAME TO WRITE THIS BOOK

I'm writing this book because people came into my office and cried out to me for help. The emotions that came along with their illness or injury were too strong for them. Or they went on for too long. Or they made them feel too much out of control. And these negative emotions made their lives miserable and their physical conditions worse.

I am director of the Chestnut Hill Institute, a small facility in Boston. People come here for individual, couple, and family psychotherapy, and therapists come for advanced clinical training and supervision. We also conduct research that's led to eleven books being published. The people we see are pretty much like you—basically normal people, more or less successful in most parts of their lives, but finding there's some difficulty that has them stumped. And they're smart enough to go for help.

A number of years ago I started noticing the degree to which physical illness or injury creates significant emotional fallout. (Perhaps I was especially tuned in to this because of what I'd gone through personally.)

Here are a few examples of what I saw. A man laid low with a back injury who's afraid that it may change his life forever. A woman with psoriasis—the illness itself was in a stable, manageable state but she had a lot of emotional issues around her appearance. A man with Crohn's disease who felt so betrayed by his body that he had little capacity to trust anyone or anything. A woman struggling with anxiety as she tried, after age 38, to have her first baby, putting herself through one difficult, risky procedure after another in the hope of getting pregnant and bringing a healthy baby to term. A man struggling with chronic shoulder pain from falling off a ladder at work. And on and on.

It began to dawn on me: maybe everyone has significant emotional issues when something goes wrong with their body. If so, I felt this was a damned shame. It's bad enough when something goes wrong physically; it adds insult to injury that our psychological selves can be so profoundly affected. The body and the mind shouldn't be like two shmoes paired in a three-legged race, where when one falls the other is brought down too. The body and the mind should be a real team—when one falters, the other should always be there to lend a hand. Unfortunately, as you and I know, it usually works the other way. The body falters, and the mind goes into a tizzy.

Although it's just beginning, there's growing recognition that emotions must be put at the heart of health care. For example, there is a growing number of studies in peer-reviewed journals giving evidence that depression, anxiety, and anger (each of which I deal with in this book) hurt the heart. Here's just one instance: heart patients who are depressed have increased risk of blood clots. By learning to understand and deal with the ways your illness or injury makes you depressed, you can decrease your risk of blood clots. On an even more fundamental level, the International Association for the Study of Pain defines pain as "an unpleasant sensory *and emotional* [italics added] experience associated with either actual or potential tissue damage." How much more should we include emotions when we look at the other dimensions of injury or illness.

I felt it was important to understand this emotional fallout. It was clearly distressing in itself. But I noticed that it made people's suffering much worse, and it seemed to prolong their condition.

SUCCESS STORIES

There weren't a lot of practical suggestions in the literature about this. New research was called for. So I rolled up my sleeves. Our approach to research at the Chestnut Hill Institute is based on the idea that if there's a problem lots of people have, there must be some who have hit on ways to overcome that problem. If we can just find them and learn from what they're doing, we can all benefit.

As I searched, I discovered many wonderful things. I saw instances of people who had learned to deal effectively with their fear that that they wouldn't be able to manage their pain. With their anger at doctors they believed had let them down. With their depression over a changed sense of what their future would hold. With their stress at not being able to deal with a spouse they felt "just didn't understand what they were going through."

Their initial emotional response was unavoidable. It's what illness or injury does to us. But their way of dealing with it set them apart.

With a process of interview and analysis I was able to pull together everything these people did to manage their emotional fallout so well. I saw what these people said to themselves and others to get comfort. I saw how they shifted their perspective to create positive emotions. I saw what they did to manage their situation so they would be less overwhelmed by what was happening. I saw the new ways they came up with for dealing effectively with their caregivers and doctors.

Then I looked for ways to translate what I learned into ways to help people feel better fast, and I tested them and selected the best ones. Finally, I distilled and organized it into the kind of help people can get from a book.

This help has one overwhelming advantage. We know

that it works with everyday people under the conditions of everyday life.

People often ask me, "What tradition or school are you promulgating?" I understand why people ask this. They want to know where I'm coming from. I'd want to know that too about anyone who was helping me.

I worship at the altar of What Works—the tradition of pragmatism. I try to empty myself of pre-existing attitudes that would stand in the way of my honestly assessing the effectiveness of any tool or technique. I'm open to every approach that's demonstrated its ability to help people. This includes a variety of mind/body techniques such as meditation and mindfulness, tools that have grown out of cognitive therapy, approaches that look at the influence of a person's context on how they feel, and many others. It also includes Eastern and Western, spiritual and scientific approaches.

Whatever your beliefs are, you should assume that the material here reflects everything of practical value growing out of those beliefs.

PERSONAL MEDICINE

This is the best time in the history of the world to get sick or injured. Diseases can be cured and injuries healed at a rate never seen before. It wasn't that many years ago when top researchers were saying they could foresee no AIDS cure. Today people with AIDS are routinely living normal lives, at least in the developed world. It used to be that ninety percent of children with leukemia died. Today nine-ty percent of children with leukemia will go on to live a long life.

So let's be grateful for the miracle of medicine today. But the job isn't over. Another whole avenue needs to be opened up. Understanding our emotional reactions to being sick or injured makes possible something I've long dreamed of: a way of approaching you when you're sick or injured not just as a body part, not just as a whole body, but as a whole person.

I call this *personal medicine*. As one man said, "My doctor needs to see the person inside me beyond my illness." He's talking about something that goes way beyond your doctor knowing your name. He's talking about a truly personal medicine, and that goes much deeper.

We've all had the experience of going to a doctor and feeling that the encounter was shallow, hollow. We may believe the doctor cared. And she might be friendly as all get out. But there was something deeply impersonal about the encounter. All you were was a moving van for bringing your body into the examination room. It was all about the body. Too many physicians act like veterinarians with patients who can sue them. (Although you'd be surprised how many veterinarians are sensitive to animals' emotional needs.)

If you were treated as a person and not just as a body, wouldn't it be your emotional life that would share the attention? Obviously we want the doctor who's trained to deal with the body to address the physical problem that started all the trouble. But unless the other part of who you are as a person is included, your emotional self, how can you possibly feel seen or feel helped or have a chance at the fullest, fastest recovery?

For example, if you've checked into the hospital for a relatively minor operation, you'd like your anesthesiologist to ask you about more than what you're allergic to. You'd like him to ask you about your anxieties related to receiving anesthesia. If this is an operation designed to help with a problem you've been trying to overcome for a long time, it would be great if your surgeon talked to you about what's making you hopeful and what you're feeling discouraged about. If there are setbacks during the recovery period, or even if the recovery period just goes on for a long time, you'll probably be relieved if someone talks to you about what's making you angry.

But we can't wait for all the doctors to change, although some are starting to change and a few have always understood the importance of emotional fallout. All we can do now is take responsibility for dealing with our own emotional issues. For now, personal medicine begins with us.

HOW THIS BOOK WILL HELP YOU

The emotional state you're in may seem like a huge vague swirl, but in reality it's made up of very specific emotional issues. And I'll help you deal with every question and concern that affects your emotional state.

I'll show you . . .

- how to feel less helpless and more hopeful and effective overall.
- how to understand the emotions that are churning through you and gain some control over your painful emotions.
- how to cope with your symptoms and gain relief from them.
- how to deal with your concerns for your future and all the other fears that might come up as a result of your illness or injury.
- how to directly help yourself feel better and increase your emotional energy.
- how to make the best possible decisions for yourself about the care you're getting.
- how to feel taken care of and make sure that you get optimal treatment.
- how to get the most out of your doctor and the people in your life who are supporting you.
- how to use your spirituality to speed your recovery.

I'm not going to leave your side until you're feeling better.

For each question or concern you have, I'll show you why you've been having the feelings you've had. Then you'll be given clinically tested tools and techniques to manage or overcome what you're dealing with.

You don't have to do more than just read this book. But the more you use what you discover here, the better you'll feel.

The Missing Ingredient in Your Full Recovery

For one thing, you will feel much better while you're sick than you would have otherwise. This makes sense. If a large part of feeling rotten when you're ill or injured comes from your emotions, a large part of feeling better will come from dealing with your emotions.

Here's another benefit. Your overall recovery will proceed much faster. There are countless documented ways that changes in the way you feel create changes in the way your body functions. For example, positive feelings and a sense of control minimize stress, and lowered stress is definitely associated with better medical outcomes. But these effects also work more directly on the physiological level. It's as if your very blood itself, and your brain and your heart and other vital organs, need you to feel at your best emotionally. But you have to deal with your emotions to avail yourself of these positive effects.

And your overall recovery will reach a significantly higher level. That's because people who are active, motivated, and hopeful about their progress work harder and smarter to achieve physical recovery, and their work pays off. Just ask clinicians. They will echo this point from their own experience: positive, proactive patients accelerate recovery. And overcoming emotional fallout helps you become a positive, proactive patient. But negative emotions create poor compliance. Here's an example of how important this is. According to the March 2004 Cleveland Clinic Heart Advisor, poor compliance is one of the top seven factors responsible for cardiovascular deaths.

We all deserve the satisfaction that comes from achieving realistic goals. So it's important to understand that recovery does not necessarily mean becoming as good as new. Lots of times that's possible, but lots of times an illness or injury takes something away from us that we'll never get back. (A woman might be able to walk just fine after a bad tumble while skiing, but her skiing days may be over.)

But we don't need perfection to feel happy, healthy, and whole. *Recovery means achieving the highest level of physical* and psychological *functioning that's possible for you given the reality of what happened to your body.* And this means that almost everyone should be able to look forward to their own recovery.

2

How Illness and Injury Create Emotional Fallout

Maybe you're wondering where all the heightened emotions I've been talking about come from. After all, it could be that when you're sick or injured your body absorbs all your attention and there's no room left for emotions. Why is illness or injury actually such an emotional event for us?

THE SECOND ILLNESS

Our negative emotions aren't mere incidentals, like a kind of lint you pick up in the process of getting sick. They are part of an organic process, and that's why I call them *the second illness*. The second illness consists of the inevitable and powerful emotional responses people have to their physical illness or injury and to the circumstances surrounding it. It's an *illness* because it arises out of a perfectly natural process that can hurt you badly if it gets out of control. It's the *second* illness because it always follows your first physical illness (or injury).

There's nothing mysterious about it. If you even think to yourself, "Oh, *shoot*," when you feel a cold coming on, the frustration and anxiety and discouragement represented by that "Oh, *shoot*" is the second illness in its mildest form.

Yeah, I know, you need a second illness like you need a hole in the head. One illness or injury is enough already. But, hey, diagnosis is the key to cure. If you want to get better, you gotta know what ails you.

According to current estimates, emotional and psychological distress accounts for at least *sixty percent* of the total distress we feel as a result of an illness or injury. This says something quite amazing. Something has gone wrong with your body physically, and yet *most* of your feeling bad lies in the full gamut of your emotions—everything from severe depression or anxiety to being mildly cranky (and everything in between).

And there's got to be a lot of the second illness going around. After all, it accompanies every one of the tens of thousands of different primary illnesses or injuries that affect people.

UNDERSTANDING
THE SECOND ILLNESS

To understand where the second illness comes from, think of it like this. When you get sick or injured, it's as if you've been kidnapped by some alien, sick body. Now how would you feel if you really were kidnapped?

For one thing, you'd be stressed out big time. *What are they going to do to me?!* We get stressed out from being stuck in traffic. How much more if you were kidnapped.

You'd also be seriously bummed out. There you are being held at gunpoint in some remote cabin. You have no idea where you are or how long you're going to be here. You don't even want to imagine what might happen to you. All you know is that you used to have some control over your life, and now you have no control at all. It's hard not to feel more and more discouraged with each passing day.

Now exactly the same thing happens to us emotionally when we get kidnapped by some illness or injury. You're seriously stressed. After all, your normal life is just as stressful as it was before. But now on top of that you've got this scary, painful, confusing medical problem that forces you into all kinds of situations you're not used to dealing with.

And you're discouraged. You weren't planning for something to go wrong with your body. Just when you needed things to go well in your life, things suddenly went very badly. Plus you're faced with something you can't fix. This isn't your area of expertise. You feel overwhelmed.

These different emotional reactions add up to what I

call *the stress/discouragement response*. Something goes wrong with your body, you feel overwhelmed, and so stress and discouragement have you in their grip. Whatever's wrong with your body keeps on, minute by minute, day by day, stressing and discouraging you still more.

Both stress and discouragement have deep evolutionary roots. That means that at least historically they've both had their uses.

Stress can be a mobilizer. It gets you going (like when you were in college and stress finally started you working on a paper the night before it was due). Discouragement can be a switching agent. When you run into an obstacle, it helps you turn from a less rewarding to a more rewarding channel (like if your poor chemistry grades helped you realize in college that you weren't cut out for pre-med and you switched to a business major).

But these days stress and discouragement—like the genetic program to put on fat that served our ice-age ancestors so well—are generally counterproductive. And that's okay, because fortunately they can be overcome.

Stress and discouragement arise from your feeling *helpless*. You feel that you have no control over things, that you're surrounded by uncertainty, that you're under pressure you can't deal with. Stress and discouragement become a problem when your emotions get mobilized but you don't know what to do, and when you feel you want to make changes but you don't know how to make them.

Instead of these negative emotions leading to their own solution, they just build on themselves and overwhelm you. One of the worst things that can happen as emotional fallout builds up is that it makes you stupid. We've all said, "I'm too upset to think." You don't just feel stupid—the stress and fear and discouragement pile up and actually make your thought processes work less effectively.

And this happens because when you're sick or injured, like when you're kidnapped, you're caught in a situation where you feel there's not much you can do. It's your sense of helplessness, conscious or unconscious, that's the root cause of the second illness. But you can reverse it.

OVERCOMING THE STRESS/DISCOURAGEMENT RESPONSE

Everything you do to feel less helpless—and there are many things you can do and will learn from this book—will help you conquer the second illness. This is the basic principle of personal medicine:

> *Everything you do to feel less helpless will make you recover faster and feel better overall.*

You don't have to be perfect. You don't have to solve every problem. You just need some solutions that address what you're going through, and then you'll feel less helpless. And you're on your way to feeling better fast.

Think of it like this. Imagine there's a little guy tucked away in a corner of your brain. Think of him as the "is-everything-okay? guy." He's up there watching you go through your life. Naturally problems come up for you, as they do for all of us. Now the is-everything-okay? guy doesn't expect things to go perfectly. But what really worries him is when he sees you losing your sense of effectiveness. In his own dumb way he goes "uh-oh" and starts churning out stress and discouragement. *Because that's the best way he can think of to mobilize you when everything's not okay.*

But you can make him turn off the stress and discouragement faucet. All you need is to do something to empower yourself. You don't have to make the problem go away. You just have to show the is-everything-okay? guy that *you're* on the job. Then *he* can go back to taking a nap.

Just remember: the is-everything-okay? guy doesn't need to see that you've eliminated the problem. He just needs to see that it doesn't make you feel helpless.

The key to dealing with the second illness is feeling that you have a little more control over what's happening to you, a little more power to influence what's going on in your life. When you get that sense of control, then stress and discouragement become self limiting. And so the second illness quickly leaves you.

Here's a little summary of how all this works:

- You get sick or injured
- This overwhelms your ability to cope emotionally
- You start feeling helpless
- This creates the stress/discouragement response (S/DR)

- The S/DR feeds on itself and takes over: this is the second illness
- If you address the emotional fallout, you will stop feeling helpless
- This will block the S/DR
- You will feel better and stronger emotionally
- Overall you will feel better sooner and recover faster.

This mechanism explains why some people aren't affected by the second illness. For example, faith gives you the sense that you're not alone, that there's someone who will listen to you and accept you, that there's an extra reason to be hopeful, and that there are things you can do (such as pray and ask someone from the clergy to visit you) that will give you a greater sense of empowerment. All this helps you cope better with illness or injury by helping you feel less helpless and more effective at taking care of yourself.

Anything you do to feel less helpless and more effective at taking care of yourself will help you cope better with whatever is wrong with your body.

TAPPING YOUR POWER SOURCE: YOUR NINE POWERS

While it's normal to feel helpless when something goes wrong with your body, there's no real *need* for you to feel helpless. Yeah, I know how easy it is for this feeling to creep up on you. But your sense of helplessness is largely an illusion. The reality is that you have the power within you to overcome your helplessness, and then you'll overcome your emotional issues and get well.

Obviously, when something goes wrong with your body, physical forces take over that you have no ability to control. That's why you feel so helpless! But while there may not be much you can do in the face of one part of your life that has changed—you really are stuck in a wheelchair, you really are too weak to go back to work—you can still feel empowered when it comes to every other aspect of your existence.

This book is filled with specific suggestions. But they rest on a foundation you already have within you. I call this foundation *the nine powers*. I want you to be aware of them so you can see how much power you have right from the get-go. And when you realize what all these nine powers add up to, you'll see that you're almost unstoppable.

TAPPING YOUR NINE POWERS

1. You know yourself. You may take it for granted, but you know the thoughts in your head, you know how you feel, you know what you want. No one can tell you what's going on with you better than you can yourself.

2. You know your life. No one else knows your life as well as you do, do they? You know the problem areas, and you also know all kinds of hidden resources. Because you know your life, you have the power to get what you need from your life for yourself.

3. You can say no. When we get sick or injured, everyone starts telling us what to do—medical people, friends, family. Well, so what? You may choose to go along sometimes, but you can always say *no*. You're not under any obligation to agree with any diagnosis or go along with any treatment until you feel ready and until you feel it's right for you.

4. You can ask questions. When something goes wrong with their bodies, people frequently say that they feel in the dark. You don't know what to expect, what to do to help yourself, why your doctor's telling you to do something, why your spouse is acting weird. But you do have the power to ask questions no matter what's going on, and this is the power to turn darkness into light.

5. You can ask for help. When you're sick or injured you need help, maybe a little, maybe a lot. No one knows what you need better than you do, and no one knows how badly you need it. If you realize how powerful you are when you ask for help, you'll see that people are ready to give you what you need, beyond what you ever imagined.

6. You can get information. Here's another power: whatever information you need, someone's got it and you can get it. Whatever you're in the dark about, someone has spent a lifetime studying it. All I can say is, thank God for the Internet. Thank God for libraries. Thank God for bookstores. Thank God for the telephone. It's all there for you.

7. *You've got determination.* You don't need to be a hero. All you need is what you've got—the ability to keep on keeping on. If you don't like your doctor, there's always another. If one treatment's a dud, you can move on to the next. If someone you're counting on doesn't come through, you can hang in there until you make him understand what you need. Your determination means it ain't over until you say it's over.

8. *You have imagination.* For some of us, imagination is the ability to visualize. For some it's a kind of memory. For some it's a dose of creativity. For all of us it's the ability to use our minds to go beyond what is and discover something new. In whatever form you have this power, you do have it, and it can help you discover possibilities that are invisible to others.

9. *You're practical.* We all have beliefs and attitudes. Some of us believe in alternative medicine. Some of us believe in Western medicine. But beliefs and attitudes never actually cured anyone. The *reason* we have these beliefs and attitudes is that, deep down, we are all committed to understanding what works best and then using it to help ourselves get better. Deep down, we're all pragmatists, and this gives us the power to uncover the treatments and solutions that work best for us.

All right, then. Let's get started helping you feel better.

3

Understanding Your Unruly Emotions

When people get sick or injured, new bodily challenges create new emotions, and we often don't know what they mean or how to deal with them. When we make sense of these new emotions and find new ways to heal them, we'll feel better fast.

Most of the time our emotions make sense to us because the things that happen to us fall within predictable bounds. You arranged to meet someone for dinner at seven, and there it is seven-thirty and he hasn't shown up yet. You're sitting there like an idiot and you're mad. To make matters worse, you know perfectly well that this person's usually late. That's partly why you're so mad. "Here he goes again," you say to yourself. Some of your anger comes from the very predictability of the whole thing, and with yourself for getting caught yet one more time.

The whole thing is upsetting, but on another level it's completely understandable. You know exactly what you're feeling and you know exactly why. In a way, this predictability is comforting. There's a strange kind of safety in living in a world where the things that upset us are utterly familiar, like the stupid drivers we know will piss us off on the way home from work.

But when we fall ill or hurt ourselves, we become a little like Alice in Wonderland. We've slipped down the rabbit hole into a brand-new world in which nothing is familiar and everything is weird. Just remember how you felt when you first realized what was wrong with you. Maybe you learned about it in your doctor's office. Maybe it hit you when you woke up to find yourself lying on the floor somewhere. It was a sense of unreality. On some level *you didn't know how to feel*. All the familiar anchor points of your life had been lost.

And yet we have all kinds of feelings anyway. It's just that we don't understand these feelings or know what to do with them. Maybe you have lots of good friends, and yet you find yourself feeling incredibly lonely. What's up with that? Maybe you have a good life, and every prospect of a full recovery, and yet you find yourself overwhelmed with sadness. Where's that coming from? Maybe you've always been sustained by your faith, but now you find that you can't stop being mad at God for letting this happen to you. What's going on here?

Right off the bat let me offer you some reassurance. Unless you were crazy before something went wrong with your body, you're not crazy now. As bizarre and inexplicable as your emotional state might seem to you right now, it's probably normal. What's happened to your body is unusual to you but it's happened to thousands or millions of other people and they've all had emotional responses similar to yours. So what's going on for you is that you're having a normal response to something quite new and unfamiliar.

But you still have those emotions, and they are tough to deal with.

Before I talk about the specific emotions you may be dealing with, let's take a step back. We need to understand what emotions are if we're going to understand how to deal with them.

THE STORY EMOTIONS TELL

Let's say that you've just had a long, incredibly trying day at work. Your day was filled with stress, but most of the problems ended up being solved rather nicely. You get home, walk in the house, sit on the bed . . . and burst into tears. You're suddenly feeling a flood of emotions, and it feels like a tremendous release. If you analyze all the specific feelings that make up this emotional state, you'll see that the feelings are all about various needs you've had and about what happened to your needs. You felt relief at the needs that were met. You felt frustration at the needs that weren't met.

So in general, positive or negative emotions are about needs. We have emotions because we have needs. If you never had any needs, you'd never have any emotions.

Positive emotions—happiness, relief, pride, affection, and others—are statements about the satisfaction of a need. It's late Sunday and you're sitting at home after a choppy weekend. Suddenly you're filled with a sense of happiness. What's that all about? Why would you suddenly be happy on a Sunday evening? Well, maybe you've really needed this quiet time. A need has been satisfied, so you feel a positive emotion.

Negative emotions—anger, fear, sadness, and others—point to a need that's not yet been met. Now if you just want to feel those negative emotions, don't worry about meeting a need. There's no law against negative emotions.

But if you're sick of the pain, then saying to yourself, "What do I need?" is the first step towards feeling better.

When we start thinking of what we need as we experience some negative emotion, many of us draw a blank. Or else we come up with some need that's impossible to satisfy. This is why so many people say it's too hard, too painful to think about what they need. But this is like saying you can't get out of the parking lot because you've come up to a speed bump. If you take your time, you will be able to think of something you need that you can get and that will help put your negative emotion behind you. Even if all you need is some time to be left alone to heal.

Just imagine that the wisest Zen master or the holiest spiritual advisor in the world had ordered you to meditate creatively on the very question "What do I need?" Now you would totally expect that it might take you time to find the answer. All right then. Be patient with yourself. Sit through the period where no answers come to you. Sit through the period where the answers all seem impossible. If it were that easy, you wouldn't be stuck with painful emotions in the first place.

But trust this. The part of you that has the feeling knows what you need. With a little time and patience you will identify some needs that are connected to this feeling. The connection may not seem logical. It's just that whenever you tune in to that feeling, you come up with this need. Accept that this is your need if it keeps being associated with your feeling.

Don't reject your need because you don't understand it or know what to do about it. Our needs usually appear to us in an unhelpful, abstract, general form. "I just need to feel safe." "I just want to be happy again." Now say to yourself, "All right, what's one specific thing that would go towards meeting that need?" It's when you get specific that you have a chance of meeting your needs.

Don't worry that what you come up with might sound too specific. "So I get a dog—that might help a little, but how will it make me feel completely safe?" There's no magic bullet that will take care of a general need. But it's precisely by getting specific that you have a chance of making progress.

Now all you have to do is *start* trying to get those needs

satisfied. The fact that you're facing those needs, the fact that you're trying to meet them, is all your inner self needs to stop feeling so helpless. You'll be amazed at how quickly you'll feel better.

Tim, 31, was a handsome guy who'd dated an awful lot of women. Then he found out he had genital herpes. He was particularly upset about this because the woman he'd caught it from had cheated on him. Herpes was a horrible climax to a dreadful relationship. Now he was starting a new relationship and was beginning to seriously fall in love. He hadn't yet told his new girlfriend about his herpes, although he felt very guilty about not telling her, and he kept vowing every day that he would tell her that night. Then she found a prescription for acyclovir, confronted Tim, heard his confession, and broke up with him on the spot.

This is an important story for the simple reason that it shows a truth about almost all illness or injury. The negative emotions we feel come largely from the way our illness or injury affects our life, not directly from the illness or injury itself.

In Tim's case the negative emotion that hit him was loneliness. There was absolutely no one in his life he felt he could talk to about what he was going through and he didn't feel he could start a new relationship. For months he just suffered with no hope of relief. He didn't know what he needed. And if you'd forced an answer from him, it would've been that he needed not to have herpes so he could find someone to love.

He went for his six-month checkup, and his doctor

asked him how he was doing. "Fine," Tim said, but his doctor could tell that Tim was covering up a deep sadness. Tim was lucky to have a doctor who was willing to push a little bit in the emotional realm. Finally Tim confessed dramatically, "I'm very lonely," as if this were a terminal disease.

What Tim didn't know was that his doctor had gone through a divorce about a year earlier and was very sensitive to the issue of loneliness. He said, "You know, loneliness is just a sign that you need people in your life. Just think of it like a vitamin deficiency. You're suffering now, but if you give yourself two good doses a day of vitamin P-for-people, your loneliness will go away." They talked some more and Tim finally saw the light. His loneliness was not an emotional disease. It was just a need he could satisfy by having some human contact with real people.

Now, I've been practicing psychotherapy for over twenty-five years. I've seen every combination of emotions you can imagine. But I've never seen a negative emotion that can't be made more manageable by discovering the underlying need and doing things to try to satisfy it.

So Tim stopped focusing on his need to be in love, which would certainly never be satisfied anyway by his staying home and feeling lonely. Instead he saw that feeling lonely was an expression of his need for human contact. So he made a point of calling friends, getting together with acquaintances, and generally doing things where he'd meet people. And his second illness was cured.

Often when we try to identify the need that underlies a negative emotion, the first thing we see is a need that seems like it can never be satisfied. This need is usually for time to be reversed and the thing that happened to be undone. Well, good luck with that! You can take any problem and define it in a way that it can't be solved. This is hurtful. If you find yourself stuck here, say to yourself, "How can I look at this problem so that I can eventually find a solution?"

When Tim said his problem was that he needed to be in love, he was defining it in a way that prevented a solution. Love is not something that you can go out and make happen. Not directly. Defining his problem as needing to be with people turned it into one that could easily be solved. Hey, there are people everywhere.

"What's really real?" Negative emotions are about something else besides an unmet need. They're also a statement about what you think is real. Notice I said, "what you think." This is important, because when we're in the grip of a negative emotion, what we think is real is usually neither the truest nor the most useful way to view reality.

So just the way it's important to ask yourself, "What do I need?" you also need to ask yourself, "What's really real here?"

There's a funny relationship between negative emotions and our view of reality. The emotion seems to confirm the reality. So if you've gotten really sick and then you get depressed thinking, "I'll never feel good again," in a strange way the depth of the depression makes it *seem true* that you'll never feel good again.

But this is upside down, backwards, and wrong. Emotions don't validate anything. They just *are*. And emotions certainly don't validate the reality they're supposedly about. *Reality* validates reality.

So no matter what emotions you're dealing with, they are based on your view of your reality. If you want to feel better, maybe you need a view of reality that's just a little more . . . real.

So I'd like you to imagine that the wisest guru living in the deepest cave on the highest mountain has said to you, "Things just aren't as bad as you think they are. Your job is to find out *how* your reality is better than you've been assuming it is. This I know is possible. Go and do it."

I also know this is possible, even though I don't live in a deep cave on a high mountain. I know it's possible, because I see people finding this more positive, more real reality all the time.

Jenny took a spectacular fall onto her elbow while out rollerblading. Her doctor seemed almost cheerful when he told her, "Well young lady, no more tennis for you."

"So when will I be able to play again?" Jenny asked.

"You don't get what I'm saying," he said. "Your tennis days are over. When you fell and smashed your elbow, that was the end of tennis for you."

Jenny was in mourning. Tennis was her favorite thing in the whole world. She just did the rollerblading because her friend liked to do it. It wasn't fair! If she hurt herself rollerblading, it should have made it impossible for her to go rollerblading anymore.

The negative emotion that most afflicted Jenny was jealousy. It was an unfamiliar emotion to her, but she was in unfamiliar territory. She was jealous of everyone she knew who did anything they liked. She hated herself for feeling this way, too, because she thought of herself as a generous, open-hearted person.

As is always the case, the strength of her feelings seemed to validate her feelings. She really was this poor creature who'd never be able to do anything she liked. And everyone else really was running around out there doing their heart's desire.

Jenny was stuck for a long time until she happened to run across a TV show about Audrey Hepburn. Imagine Jenny's surprise at learning that Audrey Hepburn had started out as a dancer, that she'd injured herself, and that acting had been her fallback, while dancing was her first love. *Whoa!* Jenny thought. This opened up a whole new vista to her.

And then she started coming across more and more stories of people who were quite happy living their Plan B when something came along to sink their first choice. People who became famous runners after they'd been crushed to learn that they were too small to play football. Musicians who had careers playing instruments that weren't their first choice. Her priest shyly confessed that he'd painfully found his calling after he'd been turned down by the FBI Academy. Her father owned a small business and revealed that what he'd really wanted to do was be an anthropologist, but he hadn't felt he'd be able to support a family doing that.

At some point Jenny started seeing reality in a new way. Living your life in Plan B wasn't some tragic accident. It was the norm. It was where life really began for most people.

Her new view of reality ended her jealousy and the second illness that had come with it.

Healing your negative emotions by finding out what's really real is actually easier than you might think. Only the first step is difficult. You have to be prepared to assume that your way of looking at reality is wrong, and that can be very difficult for some people.

Let's say you're mad at your doctor because you don't feel that he likes you. Maybe that's true. But it's painful to be sick and angry at the same time. So give yourself the opportunity to look at an alternative view of your reality. Maybe he does like you; he just doesn't show it the way you'd like. Maybe he treats all his patients the same way, so you shouldn't take it personally. Maybe whether or not he likes you has very little to do with his ability to be a good doctor for you. So who cares if he likes you or not. If you want to be liked, get a dog, not a doctor.

The point is that alternative views of the reality that's hurting you are out there, and you'll find them if you let yourself look for them.

THE POWER TO FEEL GOOD

You now have a simple, effective method, based on the latest research, for dealing with negative emotions. Whatever negative emotions come your way, now you can decide what you want.

Maybe you just want to feel what you feel. Well then, you should. But maybe the emotional state you're in is a painful burden and you want relief. If that's the case, as you've seen, there are two things you have to do:

Figure out what you need. Your negative emotion is a sign that you need something. It's up to you to identify your need. Then do whatever you can to satisfy your need. As long as your identification of your need is reasonably accurate, and as long as you try to meet your need, you will start feeling better.

Come up with a more positive, more accurate view of reality. It's almost certain that your negative emotions come from a distorted view of your situation. At the minimum you could come up with a different view of your situation that would lead to more positive emotions. It just takes a little effort to find this better view.

The power to feel good lies in these two steps. They may not give you the ability to turn on a dime. They work more like a giant truck: slow to accelerate, but able to carry a lot of weight once they get going.

Now that you understand the principles, let's look at some of the most common emotional states sick or injured people struggle with.

4
Putting Negative Emotions Behind You

I want to give you some ways to counteract specific negative emotions that come up all the time when people get sick or injured. But first I want to offer a more general prescription: *Feel free to be yourself and do what you want the way you want to do it.* The point is that you shouldn't let anyone else tell you what you should do to take care of yourself. Figure out what works for you and do that.

Right now I'm thinking of two women who were both dealing with kidney failure. Both were scared, both had difficult decisions to make, both had to deal with significant discomfort. And both were urged to read books about their condition and join a support group. That's where they differed. One woman got a lot out of the reading she did and the meetings she attended.

But the other woman was hurt more than she was helped when she did the same kind of thing. The success stories she heard didn't inspire her. She had no reason to believe she would fall into the same category. And the scary stories she heard . . . well, they just scared her. What she needed was to follow her doctor's instructions and then forget about her condition the rest of the time.

There's no one right way to counteract the emotional fallout you're facing. You just have to find what works for you, and then don't let anyone change your mind.

HOW TO STOP OBSESSING

When the bull gets into the china shop, it's pretty hard for the china-shop owner to do anything besides think about the bull. Something like this happens to many of us when we get sick or injured. We become obsessed in an emotionally painful way with what's wrong with our body. All we can do is think about what's wrong with us.

One woman developed a hard-to-treat inner ear infection. She couldn't stop worrying about going deaf.

A guy recovering from open-heart surgery couldn't close his eyes for fear that he would die in his sleep.

A woman who'd severely burned her hand on the electric heating element in her oven couldn't stop agonizing over why this had happened to her.

This is all part of the second illness. Of course it's perfectly natural for a problem with your body to absorb some of your attention. But when it drains most of your attention and most of your emotional energy, then you're suffering far more than you need to.

Obsessing over what's wrong with you is a kind of soup. It's made up of different ingredients which vary from person to person. There's usually a lot of worrying. There's your focusing on the worst thing that can happen. There's what I call hyper-vigilance—an over-sensitivity to everything that's going on or might be going on. There's a kind of paranoid concern with why this happened or why it's continuing to happen. And there, floating on the top of the soup, are the inevitable croutons of self pity.

This is definitely a soup designed to give you emotional indigestion!

But you deal with it the way you deal with all your feelings. You figure out what you need. And you come up with a more positive, more accurate view of your situation.

The woman with the hard-to-treat inner ear infection? It turned out that what she really needed was more confidence in her doctor. So first she asked her doctor, "Hey, why are you having such a hard time treating this?" Her doctor gave what felt like a good explanation, but she accepted the fact that she still needed to feel more confidence in him. When her doctor suggested she consult a specialist, she did. She was vastly reassured when the specialist ended up saying pretty much the same thing her doctor had said. This stopped her worrying about going deaf, and her second illness was cured.

The guy recovering from open-heart surgery needed a more accurate, more positive view of reality. He'd been told that the operation was a success, that the by-passes were working, and that there was every likelihood of a full recovery. But he realized that hearing this was far from enough. It felt more like a dismissive pat on the head. He needed to know what the real odds were for a man of his age and condition. He needed to know how the doctor knew that the by-passes he'd gotten were working. In fact, he felt he had a million questions. When he finally got to ask them—because he insisted that his cardiologist make time for him—his fear went away.

The woman who'd severely burned her hand? As she agonized over why it happened, she realized that her fear was either that she was pathologically careless or, even worse, that on some level she'd wanted this to happen. What did she need? Not to have this view of reality! She found a practical, levelheaded therapist who talked about these issues with her. She saw that there was no need for her to blame herself for what had happened, because everyone has their share of accidents, and they're usually not signs that anything is wrong. Her agony was over.

ANGRY COW DISEASE

A physician called to refer a new patient to me. He wasn't sure I'd want to take her on. He told me that she was suffering from angry cow disease. "You mean *mad* cow disease, don't you?" I said.

"No. I mean angry cow disease. Jessica is one of these people who get really angry when they get sick." I ignored the implication that Jessica was a cow. I knew the guy, and he didn't have a mean bone in his body. He was just trying to be cute.

But he was certainly right. Lots of people get mean as a snake when they become sick as a dog. Sometimes what they feel is a kind of all-purpose anger. They're just mad in general, and they take it out on whatever happens to be in their way. Sometimes their anger is more focused. They can be mad at themselves for getting sick or injured. They can be mad at people around them for not taking better care of them. They can be mad at the stable for having let them ride a rambunctious horse. They can be mad at God.

One thing seems to be true across the board. Feeling mean like this ebbs and flows along with whatever difficulties they're facing. The worse they feel, the madder they get.

Here it's especially important to note that you can let yourself feel whatever you want to feel. If the "getting mad" thing is working out for you, good luck. You have to answer that for yourself.

Most of us, though, don't like the mean feeling that comes over us when our bodies give us trouble. We don't want to be told to stop being so angry, but we don't want to be so angry either.

What's going on here? At first glance, getting mad when you get sick seems like a strange reaction. When something goes wrong with your body, you need people to take care of you, so you'd think nature would program you to get all cute and cuddly, the way babies are cute and cuddly. But actually, when babies aren't feeling so good, they get angry too. We think that crying equals sadness, but anyone who thinks a crying baby is sad doesn't know babies. Crying babies are furious.

And so are we when we get sick or injured. Here's the reason. There you are feeling a lot of needs you don't usually feel. Plus you're helpless to get those needs met. Plus you're impatient, because illness and injury scrape away that protective layer that enables us to maintain our patience.

Well then, needs plus helplessness plus impatience equal frustration. When you look at this equation, you can see how even a bad cold can make you mad as a wet hen. And who wants to be a wet hen?

So what do you do about it? After all, you do have needs, and you are helpless, and impatience is a real thing. See . . . I almost slipped that one by you. You're *not* helpless unless you're an infant. *Never think you're helpless.* And that's the key when it comes to getting out of the angry state you find yourself in. Instead of focusing on the ways you're helpless—you can't move because your leg hurts whenever you put any pressure on it, or you start feeling nauseous whenever you put anything in your stomach—focus on finding ways to help yourself.

Maybe it is hard for you to keep any food down. But what about just one cracker? Half a cracker? A little tiny piece you break off the corner of the cracker? Every little accomplishment takes away from your sense of helplessness. But the psychological effect vastly outweighs whatever it is you actually accomplish.

Just look at people going through rehab because of a serious injury. For some of these people standing up for the first time for even five seconds is a big accomplishment and, more important, *feels* like a big accomplishment. And that's how we should approach whatever limitations and frustrations we face coming from whatever is wrong with us.

For example, it may be that it's hard for you to get comfortable. It feels like whatever position you're in is soon a problem. Well this is a perfect recipe for need plus helplessness plus impatience equaling frustration. But now suppose you focus on the ways you're not helpless. Maybe you can take more medicine for your discomfort, or a different kind of medicine. Maybe there are new ways to get comfortable you haven't tried. Maybe you can work out a compromise schedule where you change your position every ten minutes, so that the discomfort never gets too bad, but you're not tossing and turning all the time either.

I'm not just telling you to "think positive." But the truth is you have to think about something. And if you use your precious brain energy to focus on ways of being less helpless, your overall level of frustration will go way down.

And what about impatience? It isn't always bad. In its first appearance, it may be your best signal that a real need of yours isn't being met and that you need to take action. If you've phoned your doctor because you think you've taken a turn for the worse, and the assistant says, "The doctor will call you right back," and an hour goes by, then another hour, and you start feeling more and more impatient, well, don't just sit there, do something.

You're the one responsible for your feeling helpless in this case, because you're the one who isn't doing anything. If you keep calling and ask to speak to someone in authority and let them know clearly how serious your situation is and demand to know why someone can't call you back at the earliest possible moment, you'll feel less helpless, less impatient, and a lot better.

So impatience is good if it leads to action where you can actually make things better for yourself. Then you'll feel less angry.

Lots of times, though, we're impatient but there's not a lot we can do about our situation. Traffic jams. A long line for the ladies room at the theater. A spouse that seems ridiculously inept at caring for a sick person. A broken shoulder that seems like it will never heal. It's easy to say that once you see what's inevitable, then you're an idiot to not relax and accept it. And of course we tell ourselves to relax and accept, but often that doesn't work.

That's because of fear. It's fear that fuels impatience when impatience itself seems to make no sense. You know you should just accept the long line for the ladies room *but you're afraid you're going to pee in your pants!*

This shows how we can cure ourselves of the impatience that creates anger, which plays such a big part in the second illness. Treat impatience as a problem of fear. (Later on, there's an entire chapter on dealing with fear.)

So here comes your husband, and once again it's taken him forever to bring you a bowl of lukewarm chicken soup. Right now what you want is for him to be *wearing* that chicken soup. But your anger and impatience are making you and everyone else miserable. So find your fear and you'll dissolve your impatience.

Are you afraid that he doesn't really love you? If so, tell him that that's your concern and that bringing you hot chicken soup on time is a way for him to show his love.

Are you afraid that if things got bad he wouldn't be able to give you the care you really need? If so, talk to him about that to see if the two of you can figure out what his problem is. And consider the possibility of having someone come in to help him.

Are you afraid that you'll go through this whole illness and not get a nice hot bowl of chicken soup when you really need it? If so, make sure he understands how important it is for the chicken soup to be hot and for you not to have to wait for it.

You get the point. Once you identify your fear, it's much easier for you to deal with it. Then you end your fear, you end your impatience, your anger's gone, and you feel better.

BYE-BYE BLUES

It seems unfair, doesn't it? Something goes wrong with your body, and then you get depressed. It's like getting into a minor traffic accident, and when you step out of your car a bird drops poop on your head.

And yet it's incredibly common for people who get sick or injured to start feeling the blues. This requires a three-pronged approach. If you do all three things, you will truly feel better, and they're all very do-able. If you can't do them, then you need to consult your doctor, because depression is a potentially very serious condition.

THREE WAYS TO START FEELING BETTER

Put together an anti-depression first aid kit. Unless you have a serious mental illness, depression responds strongly to things you do to make yourself feel better. It's just that when we're blue we often can't think of what to do to cheer ourselves up, unlike being hungry, when we can always think of something to eat. So what you need to do is make a list entitled "Little things that make me happy." As so often happens when we stare at a blank piece of paper, at first maybe nothing will come to you. So to prime the pump, you might want to talk to a friend and ask, "What are some things that you know will cheer me up?"

Your friend might say, well, you like flowers. Or certain kinds of music. Or walking in the woods, in a field, or on the shore. Or going out with people. Or talking to ol' Jerry, because Jerry always makes you laugh.

Great—these are all good things to put on your list. Just keep putting down as many as you can think of. And whenever you think of something new, put that down too.

Now use your list. Whenever you feel yourself getting blue, do one of the items on your list. If that doesn't work for you, do the next item. Cycle through the whole list if you have to, until you hit on something that does it for you. Maybe the last item will cheer you up because of the accumulated impact of all the other things you've done.

This list makes sense. We're simple creatures. *Happy things make us happy.* Trust me, this observation won't win you applause at a cocktail party. But it's truer and more profound than you might think.

There's an extra benefit. When you do things to cheer yourself up, you feel less helpless. And that's the second prong of our three-pronged approach.

Attack your sense of helplessness. If you're feeling blue, it's because something having to do with your injury or illness is making you feel helpless. It could be that you feel helpless to stop the aging process, which for you is symbolized by whatever is wrong with your body. It could be that you feel helpless to figure out exactly what's wrong with you, or exactly what the best treatment is.

The good news is that everything you do to try to feel less helpless will make you feel less blue, even if what you do has no connection with what's making you feel helpless. Even if you're helpless to stop the aging process, it will make you feel a lot better to realize that you're not helpless to find a really good Chinese restaurant that delivers terrific food promptly.

Remember what you were like when you were seven? You'd find out that you had to spend all day Sunday with the family at your Great Aunt Mary's house. And you'd be in agony at the very thought of it. You walked into her house. You sat there feeling incredibly glum. Then suddenly a thought popped into your head. "Mom, can I walk down to the store and buy ice cream for everyone?" And Mom said yes! End of your depression.

When we get sad now, we're still like that little seven-year-old who can get so bummed out at things that make her feel helpless, but we can cheer up so fast if we can find something to do that makes us feel effective at getting some of our needs met.

So what you do is this. Find as many ways as you can to complete the following sentence: "I'm *not* helpless when it comes to. . . ." All you need to do is see the ways you're not helpless, and your depression will begin to lift.

One of the most important ways you're not helpless is something people often overlook. And that's the third prong of our approach.

Monitor and change the things you say to yourself.

When people are depressed, they say depressing things to themselves. I call this *depression talk*, and if you're blue you can hear it going on inside your own head. You'll hear things like, "Why bother? Whatever I do, nothing makes a difference." "Things are just going to get worse anyway." "I'm such a rotten person [and here you list in quite intelligent detail all the ways you think you're rotten]." "No one cares about me anyway."

The list of statements that constitute depression talk is long. The thing is that, when you're sad, they feel like the truth with a capital T. You're just being honest. You're just seeing what's real. So how can you know that this is actually depression talk? It's depression talk if you recognize it as a negative statement. It's depression talk if it would bum you out if someone else said it about you. Last and most overlooked, it is depression talk (even if there's a germ of truth in it) if you keep saying it to yourself over and over but there's no news in it anymore.

There's an even simpler way of identifying depression talk. It's probably whatever thoughts keep going through your mind when you're feeling particularly sad. And we know that because we know what a close relationship there is between depressed thoughts and depressed feelings.

Once you've identified your depression talk, you don't have to stop it. You couldn't anyway. No one can stop themselves from thinking about something. But it will go away when you learn to talk back to it.

There are lots of ways to talk back to depression talk. The simplest is just to say, "Okay, I see what you're up to, but it's just depression talk. You're just here to make me miserable, and I'm not going to take you seriously." Then you let your depression talk go on, blah, blah, blah, but meanwhile you try thinking about other things.

You can also learn to talk back directly. Listen to what your depression talk says. Then begin by saying, "That's not the whole truth. The truth is. . . ." And you should say this even if there's a grain of truth in your depression talk. Hell, maybe you *are* old and fat. There are old, fat people out there.

But if that's what your depression talk is saying, you can answer back by saying, "That's not the whole truth. The truth is that I have a lot of good years ahead of me, I'm not any fatter than most people my age, I have a lot of energy, I've a lot of things I want to do, and I've got a lot of good friends."

Don't worry about winning a debate with your depression talk. It's a huge paper tiger. As long as it knows that you're ready and willing to talk back to it, it will eventually slink away.

Suppose you don't feel you have any way to answer back. Ask a friend to give you things to say in response to your depression talk. For example, "I keep saying to myself that my future is blighted. I'm not even sure what that means, but it depresses the heck out of me. But I do have this medical condition. What can I say back to those words?" Eventually, your friend will come up with something that will make you say, "Oh, that's good."

Once you have things to say back to your depression talk, you're on your way. Prong three is fully operational. Just make sure you do it.

COMING OUT OF YOUR SHELL

Birds do it, bees do it, even educated fleas do it. I'm talking about going off by themselves when they get sick. If you have a dog or a cat you've surely noticed this. They just want to be left alone to heal.

It's different for people. We may want to be quiet some of the time, but for most of us, human contact is healing. And yet our injury or illness makes it harder for us to reach out to people. And frankly, it makes us less desirable as someone to be reached out to. And so you get the sense of isolation and loneliness that so often come when something goes wrong with the body.

Acknowledge that you have a need to talk to people and

for people to talk to you. This need is as important and valid as your need for any medicine you might be taking.

And do everything you can to create more contact with people, and richer contact. For example, if there are people living with you, they may be constantly popping in and out to "check up" on you. And they may be bringing things to you. But they may also be backing away from having real conversations with you, partly because they don't want to disturb you, and partly because you're not able to do such a great job of holding up your end of the conversation. So you need to let these people know that it's important to you that they take some time to sit and chat with you. They may just be chatting about everyday matters, but at least you're talking with someone.

If you're alone during the day, or if you live alone, try to arrange for people to stop by. Ask friends and relatives to phone you frequently. Even if you can't get up, don't take your isolation lying down. Call your church or some other organization you belong to and ask people there to visit or call. If you're in the hospital, ask to speak to a hospital social worker or chaplain and talk to that person about arranging for someone to come and visit with you on a regular basis. Most hospitals have programs just for that purpose.

"I FEEL LIKE I'M A BURDEN TO EVERYONE"

Even someone with a bad cold can require a lot of care. So it's easy to feel like a burden when you're sick or injured.

But this is an emotionally dangerous place to get to. Two things might happen.

You might start feeling guilty. You'll get the care you need but you'll feel bad about it. And there you have it—another ingredient of the second illness. But guilt is a more toxic emotion than people think. It's not just an abstract sense of being in the wrong. It somehow curdles your other emotions. Particularly anger. People who feel guilty get mad. The more someone feels guilty, the madder she'll get. It's as if there were something particularly unbearable about guilt, literally, in the sense that you just can't carry it around. And so you have to pass it on by being mad at someone else, in the hope that they'll feel guilty.

The other possibility is that in your attempt to not feel guilty you won't let people give you the kind of care that you actually need or deserve. This can be incredibly dangerous. Lots of people recovering from injuries or from operations have re-injured themselves by prematurely taking care of themselves when they should've let others take care of them. Women dealing with tricky pregnancies have lost their babies for just that reason.

Here's another thing that happens when guilt prevents you from letting yourself be taken care of: you'll start resenting the people who are supposed to take care of you for not doing the very things you told them not to do, because you were feeling guilty in the first place. This is yet another example of how guilt curdles our emotional world!

STOP FEELING GUILTY

Now here's my recipe for getting rid of the guilt you might be feeling over the fact that your partner has to come home from work and cook a meal for you when you always used to cook a meal for him (or whatever it is you're feeling guilty about):

If the things that are being done for you are normal, appropriate, or doctor-recommended, there's no need to feel guilty. Maybe you should feel guilty about making inappropriate requests—Beulah, peel me a grape!—but people in the early stages of recovering from a broken leg, for example, do need to have things fetched for them. If you're too weak to get out of bed, then food and drink do need to be brought to you and shopping has to be done for you, too.

You don't have to feel guilty if the person taking care of you is really paying you back for ways you've taken care of him. Or if there are ways you can take care of him in the future. Or if there are ways now or later that you can show your gratitude. Most relationships are a two-way street, and eventually things balance out.

Even if the person who's taking care of you gives you far more than you can ever repay, it's best to assume that there's a kind of cosmic balance to all of this. Maybe it's good for your partner's soul to take care of you. Maybe one day you'll be able to pay someone else back. There's a lot of balancing that goes on in the universe, and you might as well assume that you're part of it. It will help you feel less guilty.

5

Shortcuts to Feeling Better

I f it were possible for me come to you now, put a hand on your shoulder, and magically make everything all better, believe me, I'd do it. I really would. But it just doesn't work like that. When we're sick or injured we have to do our best to help ourselves. The good news is that you can do a great job for yourself. And when you do, you'll feel a lot better a lot faster.

So how do you help yourself? What does that even mean when you're someone struggling with an illness or injury?

We all have an image of the way we're supposed to act when something goes wrong with our body. We're supposed to stay cheerful and maintain a positive attitude. We're supposed to do a good job of taking care of ourselves. We're supposed to face full on and with a clear head whatever is going on with us.

But too often we feel we're letting ourselves down. This can sometimes feel like the straw that breaks the camel's back. We're already feeling let down by our body, by doctors, by loved ones, by colleagues, by society as a whole, by life itself. No wonder the second illness is such a big deal! Then the doubt takes over and you begin to wonder: how will you ever get better if you do such a poor job of taking care of yourself? A sense of helplessness emerges and it is that feeling of helplessness that fuels the fire that keeps the second illness simmering.

The good news is that you can overcome that feeling with the same techniques managers use. We learn how to manage all kinds of things by the time we become adults. Business management. Time management. Pet management. Desk-clutter management. Kitchen management. So why *not* learn self management? After all, what's closer to you than your self? It's easier than you think. What's more, it's an important tool you can use to help move you along the road to recovery.

Let's deal with the most important issues that come up in self management for someone who's sick or injured.

ARE YOU HAVING FUN YET?

The men in the white coats are probably going to come and get me for suggesting that you can have fun when something goes wrong with your body. But the truth is that to recover quickly *you need to have fun*. *The worse things are, the* more *you need to have fun*.

Fun covers a broad area. You can have fun when you laugh, but you can also have fun watching a tense thriller. You can have fun talking about absolute nonsense with a friend, and you can also have fun making cookies for a school bake sale with that friend. You can have fun rowing a boat gently down the stream gazing at the clouds, and you can also have fun learning something new, maybe even learning something quite interesting about your medical condition. Generally, it is varying combinations of pleasure, play, and doing something new that add up to fun.

Fun is the paycheck you get for being alive. If you're not having fun, you're not getting any return on your investment in living. We get married because we think it'll be more fun than staying single. We recognize that people who are both happiest and most successful are the ones who've found jobs that are fun for them. And look at what happens when work isn't fun—you need your free time to make up for the lack of fun you're having at work. Even people who work at helping others, the Mother Teresa types, stay alive and committed longest when they find genuine pleasure in what they're doing.

Here's why the ability to have fun when you're sick or injured heals the second illness. The stress/discouragement response kicks in when you feel helpless to take care of yourself. The part of your brain that's responsive to this sense of helplessness pays a lot of attention to your ability to have fun. When you do something that's even a little fun—that gives you just a little pleasure, that adds just a little play into your life, that's just slightly new—then that part of your brain finds powerful evidence that you can take care of yourself, and the stress/discouragement response recedes big time.

How to have fun when you're sick or injured. The most important thing is to *remember* to have fun. Sometimes we get so busy being a patient that we forget to have fun. But the rule is that *if you're not having fun, you're not doing it right*. I know there are plenty of times and places where it's real tough to have fun, but even at a friend's funeral you can remember the good times you shared and be happy that you had them, or you can hook up with an old pal you haven't seen in a long time and enjoy catching up and reminiscing.

If you look for opportunities to have fun, you'll see that they're everywhere. Maybe you're bedridden, but what's to prevent you from having a few friends over for a mini-pajama party or a "picnic" (assuming you're not contagious, of course!), sharing some treats, eating finger foods, laughing, carrying on. Here's another example. Every time you go to the doctor, do something that's fun for you within the limits of your ability. You're out anyway, so you might as well get yourself a treat.

The main object is to look for ways to enjoy every situation. Resolve that until you're back on your feet, you're going to make a point of doing at least one little fun thing every day and one big fun thing every week. I'm not saying that this will always be easy, especially if you're in a cast, attached to an oxygen tank, or fighting pain or fatigue. But you'll be surprised at how many ways there are to have fun when you look for them.

Some things that have always been fun for you are still going to be possible. You just have to remember to do them. For example, you always like to talk to your friends on the phone. Some people, when they get sick or injured, don't feel like doing this. They forget that once they start chatting, they'll start enjoying themselves.

You might have to rediscover activities that used to be fun for you. Maybe it's been a long time since you read books just for pleasure. You've gotten out of the habit. But if you enjoyed it once, you'll enjoy it again, and now's the perfect time.

You might have to modify ways you've been used to having fun. Let's say you love active outdoor sports like skiing or mountain climbing. But now you're in a cast. Okay, why not try walking? This would've been lame when you were in perfect shape, but you might be surprised at how much fun it can be just to walk around the block on crutches if you've been cooped up. And it's especially fun if you do this with a friend.

You might even have to come up with a new definition of what's fun for you. Maybe when you were healthy watching soap operas on TV or drawing pictures in a sketch pad would've been your definition of something that was definitely not fun. But things are different now. Who knows what you'll find fun in your current state. Don't knock it till you've tried it.

HOW TO OVERCOME FEELING OVERWHELMED

When we get sick or injured, we often can't deal with what's happening to us. We don't believe it's really happening. Our brain is in a fog about what's happening. Call it denial. Call it confusion. Call it fear. But this goes on for many of us. When I had my heart attack, I'd had a number of warning episodes of severe angina, and I knew the symptoms of angina, but until I was literally brought to my knees, I refused to believe the possibility that what was happening was anything other than heartburn.

Sometimes feeling overwhelmed happens in a quite different way. We believe what's happening all right. We believe it so much that we feel totally devastated by it. This is another way of not wanting to deal with what's happening, but this time we're doing so by getting overwhelmed, not by denial.

You have to deal with feeling overwhelmed as part of helping yourself when you get sick or injured. Here's why. You'd think that stress and discouragement lead to your feeling overwhelmed. That's partly true. But it's also true that feeling overwhelmed leads to stress and discouragement, and that's where this process brings about the second illness. If you can find ways to directly overcome feeling overwhelmed—and you can—this will help heal the second illness.

There are many things you can do.

Accept that it is normal to not want to deal with what's happening. Have you ever noticed how stressful a happy event can be? Let's say that you're driving over to a friend's house, where you know they're going to be throwing you a big birthday party. Sure, this is a good thing. Sure, you're happy. But you're also stressed. There's so much to anticipate and think about and, frankly, to worry about. How could you not be stressed?

How much more stressful it is when something goes wrong with our body. What's less welcome than that? Who would want to deal with it?

Understand how normal it is to feel overwhelmed. People feel overwhelmed when things happen that they're not prepared for, that they don't welcome, and that assault them with intense input, like the feelings and fears that accompany illness or injury. In fact, feeling overwhelmed is people's basic response to new situations. We don't see this because by the time we're adults we've had training and experience for most of everyday life. Think of how many weddings the average person goes to before they go to their own wedding. But there's no way to get training and experience for being told you need a major operation, for example.

Trust that your feeling overwhelmed will pass. It's like missing the first day of school. You just have to play catch up. Soon you do catch up, and then you stop feeling overwhelmed.

Realize that to some extent not wanting to deal with what's happening is healthy. One of the things you might have thought when you got sick or injured is, "This can't be happening to me." This is actually a healthy response. It means that you think of yourself as strong and vital and fully functioning. You think of yourself as a person, not a patient.

You should cherish this response. Now obviously, if a person doesn't take care of himself, that's a huge problem. But the impulse to say, "My disease is not me," is a healthy one.

You may feel that you can't deal with what's happening, but that's just your feeling. It doesn't mean it's true. Be wary of your own bad PR. We say, "I can't cope with this" when we really mean we don't want to cope with it. In fact, we may be doing a good job of coping.

About ten years ago Carol's knees started going bad. This was particularly alarming because she was only 34. She didn't want to face being crippled, never being able to move normally, never being free from pain. She jumped at the idea that an operation would fix her up just fine.

But the first operation wasn't a complete success. Carol was completely overwhelmed at the thought of having who knows how many more operations, even though it's perfectly normal for someone with bad knees to undergo a number of procedures.

Carol went into a state of anxiety, rage, and depression all mixed together. Her poor husband had to listen for hours to Carol talking about how devastated she was. He started getting concerned and told Carol that he was afraid she was headed for a nervous breakdown. Carol said she was afraid of the same thing. A friend came by that evening and said something surprising. "I actually think you're coping really well."

"I'm falling apart!" Carol said.

"Look," her friend said, "you're just letting it all hang out. You're very emotional over this. And you're letting everyone know about every single feeling you're having. So, yeah, it looks like a mess. But you've gone back to work. You're dealing beautifully with the kids. This is a woman who's holding it all together, who's really strong."

Carol realized she was right. We all need to do a reality check when we feel we can't cope. The emotions may be churning. And we may not be coping as well as we would if things went perfectly. But if friends and family would say that you're coping as well as can be expected, give yourself a passing grade and a pat on the back and stop worrying.

Give yourself a reward every time you take a step towards feeling better. Since feeling overwhelmed is normal and even sometimes healthy, spend less time evaluating your coping level and more time rewarding yourself every time you do something to cope. Just noticing how often you actually do cope, in spite of the way you feel, will make you feel better.

What exactly do I mean by "cope"? Coping is either an action or a thought that will soon, although not necessarily right away, make you feel less overwhelmed. Feeling overwhelmed is just that: a feeling. Coping is not a feeling. You don't have coping "feelings" to counteract feeling overwhelmed. You do coping things and think coping thoughts, and then you feel less overwhelmed.

So don't reward yourself when you feel less over-whelmed. Reward yourself when you do something to cope, because coping is always the best thing to do. These rewards counteract the second illness, because they under-line how much you're not helpless.

Your reward system can be as basic as praising yourself every time you remember to take your pills, do your exer-cises, or even get out of bed. No positive action is too small to reward. The other day I was working in my basement and banged my head. There was a lot of blood, and I got scared, but then I remembered that even minor head wounds tend to bleed a lot. This thought was a form of coping, and it deserved to be rewarded.

And when you reward everything you do to cope, you achieve a victory many times a day, and that's vital, since so many of us experience feeling sick or injured as a form of defeat.

Accept the fact that you're in mourning. Yes, mourn-ing. But how is this possible if no one has died? Well, believe it or not, every illness or injury requires some mourning. After all, you've lost something. Even with an illness as minor as a cold, there's still mourning involved in giving up a fun weekend to stay in bed with the sniffles.

The way to deal with the need to mourn is . . . to mourn. We need to go through a period of grief and self pity. It's the only way we can get to the other side. Mourning is a perfectly natural process. The key to successful mourning is to let yourself feel your feelings and express them. Eventually, you will start to heal emotionally.

Many people feel overwhelmed because they haven't let themselves go through this mourning period and come out the other side. You'll always feel less overwhelmed when you're able to strike mourning off your to-do list.

FEELING BETTER ABOUT YOURSELF

When you're sick or injured, you are a yuckier version of you. There's you, and there's you with the sniffles and a hacking cough. It's obvious which you prefer.

It's natural and predictable that when something goes wrong with your body you might find it hard to feel like a worthwhile person. Often it seems as though the things we particularly pride ourselves on are what take the biggest hit when we get sick or injured. This may be because the parts of ourselves we're most proud of are what we've come most to depend on. Maybe you always thought you had a sharp mind, but getting sick made you feel dull, bleary, and confused. Maybe you always were able to run around and get things done, but now with your bum leg you just feel so damned useless.

How do you manage yourself in a situation like this?

To stop feeling badly about yourself you have to start becoming aware of the things you say to yourself. On many all-news cable channels there's a "crawl" under the picture. This is a stream of words telling you about stuff going on in the world. Well, there's a kind of crawl of words running through our brains all the time too. If you're not doing very well these days physically, and then in addition you're feeling worthless, the root of your problem is probably what's being said in that crawl of words.

You need to go inside your head and check out what you're saying to yourself. If you find yourself thinking things like, "I used to be able to . . . ," or "I'll never again be able to . . . ," or "What's wrong with me that I can't . . . ," or simply, "I'll never be good again," stop it right now. Statements like these are hindering your progress. If you change the statements, you'll change how you feel about yourself.

I want to suggest new things for you to say to yourself so you can start feeling better fast.

"I'm entitled to this down time, and it's probably good for me." Not being able to think or move or make love or function in any of the ways you used to may seem like a small disaster, but why not think of them as small vacations? You always used to have a clear head. Now you don't. So you're taking a vacation from having a clear head. *So what?* Once your vacation is over, you'll go back to having that clear head again. Why not assume that during this bleary period you're recharging your batteries?

"I'm not in great shape now, but pretty soon I'll be doing just fine." Instead of focusing on your painfully limited present, focus on what you'll be like when you're back to your old self. We often overreact to short-term phenomena like being stuck in a traffic jam, with emotions that are more appropriate to our being stuck forever than being stuck for fifteen minutes. We tend to do the same

kind of thing in response to relatively short-term physical problems.

I'm really talking about being patient with yourself and with whatever is wrong with you. What people call patience is really nothing more than the activity of *stopping* thinking that what you're going through will go on forever and *starting* thinking about how limited or unimportant the current situation really is. Then when you're more patient, you'll feel much better about yourself.

It helps to remember that impatience is the world's biggest time waster. Instead of moving things along faster, impatience sucks you into an emotional state that prevents you from focusing on what's important, and it diverts you into activities that have nothing to do what you need to do.

"I have lots of different things that I like about myself and that I do well." When something goes wrong with your body, you're no longer able to do some things. Well, let this be a warning to all of us against making too big a deal about one single dimension of who we are. You're more than just an IQ or a pretty face or the ability to play golf.

So if some part of you can no longer function well, don't think about what you've lost. Think about how you still own the mineral rights to land with a lot of precious ore in it. You may have to find it and dig it out, but it's there. And you need to keep telling yourself that it's there. How do you know that being sick won't reveal new talents or interests?

"I know I can trust myself." When you're sick or injured, your body has betrayed you. We all feel this, and so we all lose self trust at a time like this. But feelings have a way of feeding on themselves. The fact that you can no longer trust yourself to make dinner because you're not steady on your feet can easily blow up into a more general sense that you can't trust yourself.

This is where rewarding yourself for every time you've coped comes in. It's your way of showing yourself that no matter how badly you feel about the job you're doing taking care of yourself, you're doing a good enough job. *This is what taking care of yourself looks like when you're sick or injured.* It may not be pretty but it does the trick.

So decide that you can trust yourself to know what's important. To do what really has to be done. To do a good enough job. It doesn't matter that you're not perfect.

6
Making Decisions You Feel Good About

A wise man once said, "Life is all the things you say *yes* to and all the things you say *no* to." This is true. Just look at where you are in your life. You can trace how you got here back to hundreds of times when, for better or for worse, you said *yes* to going on a date with this person and to taking this job and *no* to moving to that city and to investing in that company. In other words, your life has been powerfully shaped by your decisions.

And your getting better as fast as possible also is about the decisions you make.

Medical decisions can be among the toughest a person

faces. After all, you're not feeling well, and you don't have much information. But you need to know this: the people who feel better fastest are the ones who make as many decisions as they can when it comes to their own bodies and what happens to them. They don't let themselves float in limbo. They make decisions, and they make sure that the decisions come from them, not their doctors, not relatives, not friends. All these other people are in a position to give valuable advice but not to make the best decision.

Notice that I didn't say, "People who feel better fastest make a lot of *good* decisions." I'm just saying they make decisions. That's an important way they help themselves overcome the second illness.

If stress and discouragement come from feeling helpless, then making a decision will help a lot. That's because few things make us feel more helpless than being stuck not choosing from among the options in front of us. This paralysis creates emotional fallout. You see, when you sit there not deciding, you look like someone who's helpless. That's your PR, and the person who is most susceptible to this PR is your own psychological self. But when you make a decision, you look like you're taking charge, and that PR reassures your psychological self.

Obviously, it matters if you make bad decisions. But, as you'll see, you have everything you need to make darn good decisions, and those are plenty good enough. So don't worry about making the "best" decision. Who the heck ever knows what that is? But the more ways you exercise your power to make choices to the best of your ability, the faster and more complete your recovery will be.

To help you let go of worrying about making the "best" decision, I'll let you in on a dirty little secret. Even the best doctors don't always make perfect decisions, and they're made in a messier way than you probably want to know about. Let's just say that medical decision making is not an exact science. It's often based on a subjective sense of the probabilities and on the doctor's own preferences.

But most doctors get the job done. They accept how difficult it is to know what's best to do. But then their goal is to move forward as best they can. Fortunately, what doctors have that you don't have is rules of thumb that help them make *good enough* decisions relatively quickly.

And now here you are, as a patient, having to make your own medical decisions. Of course it feels hard. It *is* hard.

The real issue, though, is whether you have everything you need to make the best possible decisions under the circumstances. And here's where I have very good news for you. *You do.* You've made plenty of decisions in your work and in your personal life. You're willing to learn more about your condition. That's all the foundation you need.

THE RULES OF GOOD MEDICAL DECISION MAKING

The main reason people don't exercise their ability to choose is that they've lost confidence in their ability to make decisions. Has that happened to you? Perhaps you feel that you've made more than your share of bad decisions. Or perhaps the medical decisions you're facing seem so fraught with serious consequences that you can't bring yourself to step up to the plate.

But making good medical decisions is not as tough as it can seem, even when there's a lot at stake and your crystal ball is all clouded over. If you follow these simple decision-making rules, your natural common sense will carry you the distance:

Never make an important decision until you've been able to air out your situation with your doctor and with a smart friend or family member. You need to feel that you've had the time and opportunity to look at things from all angles, and you need to give smart, knowledgeable people the chance to share their thoughts with you. But if your doctor won't talk to you as a full partner in the decision-making process, get a new doctor.

Never let yourself be rushed. Give yourself time, at least overnight, to think over any important decision. (Obviously, this doesn't apply to true medical emergencies.) You need this time so you can feel confident about the choice you make. Here's a valuable tip. Use the time you've allowed yourself to make a provisional decision and live with it and see how it feels. If you've decided that you're going to go ahead and have that operation, then live with that decision for twenty-four hours before you tell anyone what you've decided. Maybe with time you'll feel more comfortable with it. Or maybe you'll realize that you're really not happy with the idea of it at all.

Don't make decisions just to please other people.
You may feel that your doctor will secretly respect you more
if you decide one way rather than another. Your spouse, parents, or kids might be actively lobbying you to make a certain decision. Look, they may have valuable information
about what's best for you that you need to listen to. But I
promise you that you won't be pleased with your decision
unless you make your decision to please yourself.

Don't be ignorant. The more information you get and
the more smart people you talk to, the more you can trust
yourself to make a good decision. It's important not to
limit yourself to information you get over the Internet.
This can be enormously helpful, but you also need experienced, informed people to help you sort through this information and put it in perspective.

Take things a step at a time. Be conservative. No, I'm
not talking politics. But the more extreme the intervention,
the greater the risks. You don't want to subject yourself to
any more risk than you need. So start with the smallest
step you can, and see what happens from there. It's particularly important to be careful about surgery. Surgeons are
wonderful people and life-saving operations are performed
every day, but surgery should only be undertaken when all
the more conservative options have been at least carefully
examined, if not tried. "Just do it" may work for going jogging, but it's not the approach to take when contemplating
surgery or any other major intervention.

Don't expect perfection. Accept the fact that all health care is a process that you know will have its ups and downs and its share of surprises. Don't get thrown if things don't work out the way you'd hoped. Approach every decision with a "let's see if this works, and if not we'll fix it" mindset. Then just keep making decisions about whatever comes up and you'll do fine.

Never lose sight of what's most important to you. Sometimes our priorities do more flip flops than a troop of acrobats. All this does is confuse us. And we get into this situation because we think it's enough to "know your priorities." But that's not enough. We *do* know our priorities. Now we have to go one step further. In every decision you face, you have to decide what your *most* important priority is. For example, is your top priority avoiding pain? Avoiding expense? Avoiding running around from one doctor to the next? Avoiding *dying*? Hey, man, it's up to you, but *you have to pick one*. You'll always make a great decision if you base it on what is truly most important to you. So make sure you have plenty of time to explore what's most important to you in the context of a particular decision.

Bottom line: You don't have to be perfect because perfect is a concept that doesn't apply. You just have to avoid these mistakes. That will clear the way to your making excellent decisions.

OVERCOMING OBSTACLES

Here's how to deal with some of the major obstacles people commonly run into when they need to make medical decisions.

"I feel like I don't have any choices." Of course not having choices is one of the definitions of helplessness, so this could contribute significantly to the second illness. And it often seems as though there aren't any choices, like when your doctor says, "That gall bladder is going to have to come out."

Not feeling helpless is so important that I'd like you to think about not having choices in a different way.

If there's really only one choice—like calling 911 if you recognize that you're having a heart attack—then this is the one time you can know for sure that you're making the best choice. But you almost always have more choices than you think. Try this. If your health-care provider says that you have to do X, say, "Well, if I don't do X, what else can I do?" If you ask questions, you'll find that there are options that you hadn't known about before. If you assume that there are options, you'll find them.

"My doctor/spouse/parent/kid keep telling me that I have to do something, but I really don't want to do it and I don't know how to stand up to him." The key is that it's your body and your life. All your doctor has to offer is some expertise about what the options are and what the most likely outcomes are from these options. This is information that can help you decide; it's not a power to take your decision away from you. As for your spouse, parents, friends, and kids—the only expertise they have is in what their own preferences are. Don't know how to stand up to them? Just keep telling yourself (and them), "It's my body. It's my decision."

It's a little different when your doctor tells you that you have to do something. First, don't automatically assume that your doctor is right. That's why a second opinion is so valuable. But instead of getting into a push/pull kind of fight, talk to your doctor about what you want to do, talk about what he wants you to do, and then *ask him to help you list the pros and cons of both options*. He has the medical expertise. You have the *you* expertise—you know yourself and your situation. As you both list the pros and cons, medical and personal, you'll either see that your doctor was right all along, or you'll have in writing in front of you all the good reasons why you should stand up to him, or you'll see that it really amounts to a coin toss or a matter of personal preference.

"I just want someone to make all the decisions for me." Of course this is how you feel. You're not well! Sometimes when we're not feeling well, we don't even want to decide what we want to eat for dinner. When I've been sick I've said plenty of times, just bring me whatever you think I'll like. But here's what happens. As my poor wife walks off to get me something to eat, I'll call after her, "I would like something cold, though." Then when she gets into the kitchen, I'll yell out, "I'd like something soft." By the time she gets back to me with some cold, soft tomato slices, I'm thinking that all I want is some ice cream right now. The point is that we want people to make decisions for us, but we also know what we want, better than anyone else. Just tell people what you want.

"I'm so totally overwhelmed by all the information there is out there on the Web about my condition, and my friends tell me a million different things—I can't even begin to sort it out to make all the decisions I have to make." Ha! You've discovered exactly why doctors hate the Web, and hate most of your friends, too. We used to live in a world plagued by ignorance. Now we all basically live in the Library of Congress. The only thing we're ignorant about is how to process all this information.

This is why you want to have an experienced doctor on your team. When your doctor started practicing, I promise you that he was as overloaded by information as you are. Experience is precisely what makes it possible for someone to look at a mess of information and know quickly how to sort the wheat from the chaff. And it's mostly chaff. But you deserve to have your information discussed seriously.

If you've come across some doctor out in Hawaii who's found a new treatment, if you've read a study based in Finland about a new diagnosis for your symptoms, talk to your doctor about it. Don't let your doctor get away with saying it's nonsense. You have a right to have it explained to you why this good-looking alternative approach really isn't so hot.

But you can do a lot of the processing yourself. The great majority of Web-based medical information is seriously marred by bias. I'm not saying that it's definitely wrong. But I am saying that the people running the site offering this information usually have a bias. For example, sites that promote "natural cures" tend to support information that supports the natural approach. They tend to downgrade or omit information that supports a more technological approach. This doesn't mean that the information they're offering is wrong. It just means that you can't assume that it's right.

The same holds true about information promulgated by drug companies, vitamin companies, sites supported by particular forms of treatment, and so on.

Some of the most neutral sites I've found, and the ones that seem to offer the best information, are sites run by organizations devoted to a particular disease or injury, like the American Cancer Society, the American Thyroid Foundation, and so on. But be careful. There are also sites that have very official sounding names that are run by people with a very strong bias.

Other excellent, unbiased sites are run by major medical schools. In addition, I've personally found that WebMD and Medscape are excellent sources of solid medical information.

7

What You Can Do to Ease Your Symptoms

We go to the doctor because our body suddenly develops a mind of its own. Whether it's pain, nausea, dizziness, weakness, or some kind of incapacity, it's as if your body suddenly started doing stuff that you really don't like. And there's nothing you can do about it.

So right away you're feeling helpless, and this quickly leads to significant emotional fallout. We're not talking about your diagnosis yet, just about your symptoms, how you actually feel, and it's at this primitive level that you have your first and best opportunity to regain a sense of control and set the second illness back on its heels.

LISTENING TO WHAT YOUR BODY'S REALLY SAYING

There is something you can do to show your body that you're here to help. It involves really listening to what your body may be trying to tell you. This is different from being hyper-aware of every twinge of discomfort. We're usually *too* tuned in to that. But if you listen to what your body might be telling you, you might learn something that will help you help your body.

Let me show you exactly how to listen to your body.

First, make a commitment that you're going to stop fighting your body. This isn't a fight you can win. Your body is going to have certain needs as you go through your illness or injury, and you'll have much less anger, stress, and disappointment if you give in to your body's needs as much as possible. If your body tells you it needs to take a short nap during the day, or maybe even a couple of naps when you're getting over something, who are you to argue?

The opposite of fighting your body is heeding your body. So sleep if you need to sleep. Eat if you need to eat. Don't eat if that's what you need. If your body tells you that certain people or situations are stressful for you, and it feels like your body wants to avoid those people or situations, let your body have its way.

On some level we're just animals. Animals don't know about medicine, but if you've ever had a pet, you know that animals listen to their bodies when they get sick or injured. And this is how they achieve a surprising cure rate in the wild, even though bears and beavers can't pop into a veterinary clinic whenever they want.

But you can take listening to your body much further, and you should. You can actually use your body as a special source of information about *you*. Somehow, in its distress, your body has come to understand things about you that you don't know. And you need to find out what those things are.

Let's be clear about what this technique is and what it isn't. It isn't a cure for pneumonia or for a pair of fractured ribs. If you want to cure your body as a body, what you need to do is listen to your *doctor*.

But this body-listening technique is something many people have used successfully to help themselves feel much better overall when faced with some illness or injury.

Here's what you do. There you are, sitting in bed or on a bus or even on the beach. Now I'd like you to pretend that you pick up a phone and dial 1-800-MYBODY. This is a direct line to . . . *your body*. It has nothing to do with your symptoms. You're bypassing them completely. What's nice is that your body will immediately answer the phone. "Hello, your body speaking. How may I help you?"

And you say something like, "No, listen, I'd like to help *you*!" Then ask your body this question: *"Body, about my illness or injury—why is this happening to me?"*

Now your body understands that you're asking for some information about *you*, how you've been living, mistakes you've been making in your life, changes you're needing to make, ways you're needing to grow, unfinished business from your past that you're needing to clear up.

That's the kind of thing you're looking for when you ask, "Body, why is this happening to me?"

Now of course your body won't literally answer you. But bodies have different ways of talking to us. Most people report that they sort of "hear" an answer in their mind. Or else they see a kind of picture that shows the answer. Or else they feel a truth emerge in their consciousness.

You can, if you want, think of this as an exercise in which you use your imagination. You ask your body what's happening to you, and you imagine a response.

To help you get a better sense of what to expect, here's what some people heard when they asked their body why a particular problem was happening to them.

One woman really did almost have a sense of her body directly saying to her, "You've neglected your body for years. What did you expect? Now you've got to take much better care of yourself." She took this as a call to visit her doctor more often when she was afraid something was wrong, to eat better, to reduce stress. In other words, to treat her own body the way she treated her children's bodies.

Another woman heard her body say, "Sure you're having chest pains—your heart's been broken a number of times. You've had losses in your life that you've never fully dealt with. Face them, mourn them, find ways to move on—that will help your body a lot." And she knew that this was absolutely right. (Of course if you're having chest pains, you must be checked by a doctor. But you're listening to what your body says to you as a way to cure the second illness and relieve your symptoms. This is in addition to, not instead of, your getting good medical care.)

One man saw a picture of himself as old and decrepit. For him this was a sign that his body was telling him that he had to start exercising vigorously and consistently right away.

One woman started crying. She suddenly felt a longing for love that she hadn't been aware of. She was married, but for years she'd neglected her own sense of how little she got from this marriage. It was as if her body was telling her, "Whatever you're going through is partly connected to the fact that you need to find love." She made the painful but necessary decision to end what she'd long known was a dead relationship. And she started feeling better the minute she made that decision.

One man experienced his body saying to him, "I just can't handle all this fear." Oh, yes, he had something real that was wrong with his body, but his fear was real too. And then he realized how much fear he was living with. When he started dealing with his fears, he started feeling better.

One woman broke her big toe. When she asked her body what it was saying, the answer she got back was, "Honey, we need a vacation." And that's how she treated her broken toe—as an opportunity for a real holiday that she'd been deeply needing in mind, body, and spirit.

You need to be patient with this process. When you ask your body why this is happening to you, you might not get any answer right away, or the answer might not be clear, or you might not know what to do with the answer. Hey, give your body a break. It's not used to talking!

Just keep asking and keep listening. If something's not

clear, ask your body for clarification. But I'll tell you this. If you keep dialing 1-800-MYBODY and keep asking questions and listening hard for answers, you will start hearing responses you can begin to act on. Make sure you act!

Action is the key. Bodies mumble—we're not always sure what they're saying to us. And we don't always know just the right thing to do in response to what they're saying. But if you listen, and make your best guess as to what your body is saying, and your best guess about what to do, *and then do it,* you'll have done a lot to feel better fast.

Of course your body can't really talk to you. It's just *you* talking to you. But this is all part of personal medicine—bringing together parts of you that have been alienated or forgotten or left out. What's emotionally true is that you really do have some need or unfinished business that your illness or injury is bringing up for you, and you'll relieve your heavy heart if you take care of this business.

On listening more deeply. It sometimes seems to people that their bodies are talking to them and saying things that are actually hurtful. Franny, 43, was a 94-pound woman who responded to stress by losing her appetite, and things were pretty stressful in her life. She might have said, "I don't have to listen to my body—it's telling me loud and clear not to eat." But Franny was smart enough to check with her doctor, and he said, "What are you—nuts? At 94 pounds you're skin and bones. I'm going to be worried about you until you get to 110."

The truth is that sometimes our bodies tell us things that aren't good for us. So how do you know when to listen to your body and when to tell your body to shut up?

All I can say is that you have to use common sense. If you're a 94-pound woman and your body tells you not to eat . . . *isn't there something wrong with this picture?* Usually when we tune into what our bodies are saying to us, the helpful answers make a kind of sense. If you've been sick or injured and your body is telling you that you need to sleep, that may not be what you want to do, but you have to admit that it passes the common sense test.

So listen to what your body tells you, but if it doesn't make sense or you're not sure, check with your doctor.

FEELING GOOD WHEN YOU'RE FEELING BAD

Our bodies are greedy little things. They want a lot more than just not feeling bad. They want to feel really good. Just think about how you'd feel right now if the world's greatest massage therapist suddenly appeared behind you and started working on your neck and shoulders. More than that, though, feeling bad is something we need.

If you can do things to make yourself feel good in ways that have nothing to do with the parts of you that feel bad, that will take a huge bite out of the stress/discouragement response, and you'll feel much better overall, regardless of what else is happening with your body.

Complete this sentence: "What would make me feel really good right now is. . . ." And I'm talking about things that will make you feel physically or emotionally good. The words "right now" are important. One minute it might be chocolate ice cream, fifteen minutes later it might be a hug. Today it might be flannel pajamas, tomorrow it might be a visit from your best friend.

Sami, 27, found herself dealing with the sinus infection from hell. For a long time it went misdiagnosed. Antibiotics and other treatments took a long time to work. When she started asking herself what would make her feel really good right now, the answer she got back revolutionized her life. Sami had always been a hard-working, duty-driven woman. There was very little in her life that felt good most of the time. The pleasurable things she did made her sinus pain much more bearable while it lasted.

Thinking about what would make you feel really good right now is the start of your taking an active role in your emotional well being. Then, as soon and as often as possible, try to bring into your life things that will make you feel good. Some of the desires that come into your head will have to remain fantasies. But many are more do-able than you might suspect. Often the barrier is our not letting ourselves believe that we really can ask for something and then really have a chance of getting it.

People who are good at dealing with the emotional aspects of their illness understand that a focus on eliminating the ways you feel bad isn't always the best approach. There are times when you've done your best, and that's that. But they also understand that feeling better can come just as much from adding new ways to feel good as from eliminating ways you feel bad.

TAKING POWER OVER
YOUR SYMPTOMS

There are things you can do right now to feel better and less helpless in the face of your discomfort. If you practice any of these techniques, you'll be surprised at your power to make yourself feel better.

Different people refer to these techniques by different names. Some call them mind/body techniques. Other people might think of them as forms of meditation. Still others might refer to them as ways of doing cognitive therapy on yourself. What's important for you is knowing that our minds are incredibly powerful, and we can deliberately use our minds (if we're shown how) to help ourselves in ways we never imagined.

As we actually live our lives, most of us feel controlled by our minds. We think what we think, feel what we feel, and we have no more power over these brain storms than we do over a summer thunderstorm. But I know for sure that at some time in your recent past you actually demonstrated that you can use your mind to make incredible things happen. Maybe you "decided" that you weren't going to be mad a someone any more, and you weren't. Maybe you were trying to fall asleep, and to help yourself you made yourself think about pleasant, happy things. Maybe you caught yourself having negative thoughts and told yourself to cut it out, and found that you actually cheered up. We often do things like this without even realizing it, *but we do them.*

Direct relief. Imagine actually being able to *dial back your discomfort*. It works a little like a guided meditation. Get in a relaxed position. As you read this, let your mind go in the direction the words suggest.

In a moment I'm going to ask you to think of a number from zero to one hundred. Zero will mean that whatever has been bothering you in your body—pain, dizziness, nausea, weakness, itchiness, whatever—has disappeared. It's not a problem at all. You're free of it. One hundred stands for the worst level you can imagine your symptom getting to.

Gaining power over your discomfort begins with your taking an exact reading of how you feel. A number, *any* number, is much more manageable than a cloud of feeling. A number is a baseline. A number is something you can work with. A number is *a beginning*.

Now tune in to your symptom and how it feels to you *right now*. Let a number come into your mind. Got it? This number will best represent your level of discomfort, pain, weakness, whatever. You're the judge of where you are right now. Just remember, one hundred is the worst, zero is the best.

Now focus on your discomfort for a few seconds. Then see whether that raises or lowers the number. You may notice, for example, that at first the number is slightly higher. No surprise really. You're paying attention to your discomfort, so the number's registering a little higher, that's all. Discomfort often seems to feel worse when we pay attention to it.

There's good news in what just happened. Even though

your number went up a little, you were the one in control. It went up because of what you paid attention to.

Now you're going to start taking a little more control, but in a way that should be easy for you.

I'd like you to imagine a scene that feels beautiful to you. It's a scene that makes you feel happy and peaceful. As you let this scene stay in your mind, try again to think of a number that indicates the level of your physical distress.

Almost certainly it's now a lower number than it was before. And why not? You have something better to pay attention to than your discomfort, and so you don't feel it quite as much.

Well, that's *it*. You've just demonstrated that you're not helpless. Sure, you probably didn't make the discomfort go away completely. But you saw that you can focus on it and make it get worse, or think of something beautiful and comforting and make it get better.

This is the beginning of your rebuilding your relationship with yourself and your body. Instead of your body always being in control, *you've shown how you can take control of your body.*

The Power of Distraction. You have the power to think of a number that represents your level of discomfort any time you want. This is a simple technique; you should use it all the time. Whenever you become aware of your discomfort, check out what the number is. Then make it go lower by thinking of something pleasurable or something that takes you outside of yourself.

One of the foundations of your ability to take control over your distress is distraction. People often talk about the power of imagery and visualization. They're right. These can be very powerful. But they get their power from their ability to turn your mind from an awareness of what's bothering you to an awareness of something else.

Let's not kid ourselves. It's not the imagery but the distraction that's the active ingredient. Sure, if your head hurts it might help a lot to imagine your head being bathed in warm, bright, healing light. But listening to quiet music might help more. Talking to a friend might help more. Don't get locked into just one approach. Keep trying different ways to distract yourself.

Keeping busy is one of the best ways to distract yourself when you're sick or injured, if you can manage it. But "busy" covers a wide range of activities. I always used to think that when I was suffering from a bad cold, taking a shower somehow magically made me feel better. What I now think is that I'd woken up and was lying in bed with nothing going on but my thinking about how miserable I felt. Even reading or watching TV failed to break the spell. But showering was such a radical shift in my activity rate that it took me out of my body, and that's why I felt better.

You may find that you have to push yourself just a little to do something that distracts you. But it's worth it if it helps you dial back your discomfort.

Turning up the power. You can dial back your discomfort even more directly. I call this technique *direct dialback*. Let's say you're feeling dizzy. Okay, but what level are you at? The number that comes to mind is, hmmmm, fifty-five—pretty dizzy. Now you're going to do something amazing. *Just imagine the number coming down to a lower reading by itself.* Focus on the number, not the discomfort. Don't make it happen. Let it happen. Relax into it. Just say to yourself, "And now the number will go down," and then let the number sink almost of its own weight from fifty-five to fifty-four to fifty-three to fifty-two and so on.

As the number comes down, your discomfort grows less and less, right along with it. Instead of the discomfort controlling the number, the number is controlling your discomfort. You'd be surprised at how often and how well this works.

There are hidden benefits. Watch what's going on in your body while this happens. You'll notice something pretty cool. You'll see that you're doing something—I don't know what it is but *you'll* know what it is—that enables your dizziness to fall back to a lower level. Maybe you're just letting it go—that's how many people describe it. Maybe you're relaxing. Maybe you're changing your position. Maybe you're focusing feelings of warmth or light on your area of discomfort.

I just know that as you imagine the number going lower and experience the discomfort getting less, there are real things you're doing to bring this about. Your job is to notice what they are so you can use them again.

Letting go. We think of discomfort as something having a grip on us. It certainly feels that way. An itch has worked its way into our skin. A pain has gripped us from the inside. Dizziness has seized hold of us. But we can reverse the way we think of this. Why not think that you're the one who's doing the holding? It's as if you'd had a grip on your discomfort without knowing it. When you relax a little, you let go of the discomfort and it flows away from you.

Think of it like this. You're standing in a stream. A lovely, friendly, safe stream of water. And you're facing upstream. You're watching the water flow towards you. And you feel the water flowing away from you behind you. And now you imagine that you relax and let go of your discomfort. As you let go, it's flows away from you with the water. And you feel better and better.

You let go of your dizziness and it flows out of you, down the stream of water. You let go of the pain in your back and it flows out of you, down the stream of water. You can do this with any discomfort whatsoever. Even if you don't feel that you're good at this technique right away, you will get better and better as you keep doing it.

I've just given you a number of exercises that allow you to take power over your discomfort. And you've proven that you have this power.

It takes practice to get good at using these techniques. And you may not be able to use them to completely eliminate your discomfort. But that doesn't matter. When it comes to curing the second illness, your sense of helplessness can diminish a great deal even if you're only able to partially improve how you feel. But you have some control now, and that makes all the difference. Remember, you've only started doing this. You should feel proud of yourself.

Keep on doing it every day. Or every hour of the day if you're in a lot of discomfort.

Now once you've experienced this, you should realize that something profound and revolutionary has happened. You had a level of discomfort going on in your body. It seemed to be in control of you. But then, using some techniques anyone can use, you discovered that *you're* in control, because you can change your level of discomfort! This small victory is a big step in curing the second illness.

8

Taking Back Control over Your Body

Let's look more closely at how your bodily sensations create emotional fallout.

Before you got sick, your old body was familiar to you. It might not have functioned perfectly. But even if you woke up tired after not getting a good night's sleep, even if you had a stomach ache from eating too much pizza, this is was all predictable and made sense to you.

But your sick or injured body is *terra incognita*—full of puzzles and surprises. Whatever's going on, you just want to make it all stop. But right now it feels like you can't make it stop.

Maybe you're in pain, and the pain is bad enough, but you're also afraid the pain won't go away, or will get worse. Maybe your back went out on Tuesday and when you woke up on Wednesday you were upset to discover that your back hurt even worse.

Maybe you feel very weak, but you also find it very depressing to be so weak. Some people find that when they're too weak to go to work they develop many of the symptoms of depression.

Maybe you're tired all the time, and you can't stop being angry with yourself for being so tired, and angry with the people around you for not understanding why you're so tired. There's got to be a lot of this going around, since almost all illnesses and injuries have fatigue as one of the symptoms.

Maybe you're confused and overwhelmed by what's going on in your body because it comes and goes and you can't figure out any pattern. Many doctors are aware of the fact that the "standard case" is rarer than you might think. And there you are, having to deal with pains and problems that don't fit the norm. How could you not be filled with uncertainty?

Well, let's put an end to this emotional fallout that comes from feeling that it's your body, not you, that's in charge.

Remember the basic principle of personal medicine: *Everything you do to feel less helpless will make you recover faster and feel better overall.*

Whatever your body is doing to make your life hard, it's time you found a way to take some control back. And it turns out that you can always do that. No, I'm not talking about waving a magic wand that makes your symptoms go away. That's not possible, but it's not what you need either.

You stop the stress/discouragement response not by becoming all powerful, but by showing yourself that there are things you can do to feel less helpless. *A small decrease in your sense of helplessness will yield a large decrease in the emotional fallout you have to deal with.* This is the leverage principle, and it works powerfully in your favor to help you overcome the second illness.

So let me show you some ways right now that you can develop a greater sense of mastery over what's happening in your body.

HOW TO STOP FEELING OVER-WHELMED BY YOUR DISCOMFORT

There's a kind of panic that sets in when you have some kind of discomfort or distress, *any* kind, not only pain but anything that happens to your body that you don't like, such as weakness, tremors, loss of function, even itchiness. This panic kicks in when the specific kind of discomfort you're feeling seems overwhelming and unfamiliar.

If you stub your toe the way I did just yesterday, it hurts like hell for a minute. But even when I was in pain, I was aware of thinking, hey, I've stubbed my toe lots of times—it does hurt a lot at first, but the pain goes away pretty fast. This was familiar pain, not overwhelming, so there was no panic. But several years ago I was straining to lift a large stone in my garden when I suddenly got an intense headache. Not only did it hurt a lot, but nothing like this had ever happened to me before. I had no way to orient myself. Instant panic.

Actually panic can arise in two ways. In one way, the discomfort gets worse and worse and you're in a panic because you don't see a limit to how bad it can get. Imagine having a stomach ache where the pains keep getting sharper and sharper, or an itch that starts in one small place and slowly starts taking over your entire body.

The other way is more insidious. The discomfort stays at the same level but panic gradually sets in as you start to wonder whether it will ever end. Let's say you hurt your back, and as the hours turn into days, nothing seems to make your discomfort go away.

Either way, the panic you feel can be pretty intense. After all, you have two conditions to deal with: your pain or discomfort and your fear about it.

When it comes to this kind of panic, the antidote is hope. You're in a panic because you don't see a boundary to your discomfort. The hope comes from having a sense of where the boundary is. Everything you do to try to find where the boundary to your discomfort lies—*and there always is a boundary*—gives you hope, which gives you more of a sense of control, which eases your panic.

When my wife was pregnant with our first child, she was *already* dealing with the second illness, because of her fear of the pain of childbirth, which was based on her fear that the pain would get worse and worse without limit.

Hope is the relief that panic's been looking for. So forget

the fear. Ignore it. Put all your energy and attention into finding new hope.

Let me tell you how to do that.

A light at the end of the tunnel. If you're afraid your symptoms are going to keep getting worse or will never end, *get more information*. That's right. Information is a kind of giant hope-making machine.

Let's go back to when my wife was in labor. There she was, her contractions getting more and more painful. Uh oh, instant panic. Now here's information to the rescue. She remembers that every mother in history has gone through this and has usually turned out fine. In fact, most of them have been eager to have another kid. She remembers that there are plenty of things that doctors can do to relieve the pain if she asks for them. She remembers that at some point a baby comes out, and then the pain ends. She remembers the childbirth classes she attended that showed her that there were limits to the pain, and gave her ways to control it.

That's a great example of information curing panic by giving hope. So here is what you need to say to yourself to deal with whatever you're experiencing in your body: "There's something I don't know yet that I can find out, and when I do, it will make me feel much better."

This might mean nothing more than talking to your doctor about the limits of what you're going through. It might also mean talking to other people who've had your condition. It might mean doing some reading.

There are three questions you need answers to:

"Can something more be done to ease my discomfort?"
Doctors will tell you that many times during the day they find themselves saying, "I can't believe you put up with this for as long as you did." I think sometimes we have an image of ourselves as whiny babies, but more often the truth is that denial and a misplaced stoicism prevent us from getting help for a lot of the things that bother us. The best medicine comes from tapping into not just experts but the whole community. The smartest thing to do is to always assume that *something* can be done about *whatever* symptoms you're dealing with, and there's someone out there who has suggestions that will work for you. Why not give yourself the physical and emotional relief that comes from getting the help that's available.

And the reason you ask if something "more" can be done is that doctors tend to assume that what's being done already is adequate unless they hear otherwise. But people often assume that what's being done to manage discomfort is all that can be done. There is almost always additional help for your symptoms.

Jennifer worked in a law office. Her job required her to type a lot. She began to notice a pain in her left forearm that got just a little worse every day. She diagnosed it herself, and she turned out to be right: carpal tunnel syndrome. It was a blow. She had an image of the pain just getting worse and worse until she'd no longer be able to work.

You can imagine what this was like for Jennifer emotionally. Your physical problem may be very different, but what's the same for so many of us is the scary sense that we're headed down a slippery slope on which the symptoms get worse and worse no matter what the cause is.

Jennifer didn't want to go to the doctor. Like many of us, she "knew" what he would say. She'd have to undergo painful and risky surgery. Or she'd have to take painkillers and possibly get addicted. Or she'd have to wear uncomfortable and unsightly arm braces. Or maybe nothing could be done.

She discovered something very different from what she'd expected. Jennifer's doctor found out that Jennifer had very low thyroid levels. He explained that in a number of cases, carpal tunnel syndrome disappears when low thyroid is treated. Just to be on the safe side, the doctor gave Jennifer other things she could do, such as exercises, ergonomic adjustments, vitamins, frequent breaks, and a brace she would only need to wear at night.

Like many of us, Jennifer had thought she knew her situation, but she was wrong. Remember, she was distorting reality precisely because she was afraid. That's what fear is—you get bad news and that distorts your sense of reality to the point where all you can think about is more bad news. You need help putting a boundary on the bad news and uncovering the possibility of good news. This is why I can say that if you're afraid that your symptoms will get worse or won't go away, information will almost certainly show you an upside and will give you new hope.

"How long will it last?" Most illnesses and injuries follow a natural course. Knowing that there's an end point will give you a lot of hope. Then, when you're feeling most uncomfortable, you can focus on that end point and it will significantly relieve your emotional distress, even if your physical distress is still with you.

So make sure you look for information or ask your doctor about the endpoint to the discomfort you're experiencing. Give your doctor a chance to show you the pot of gold at the end of the rainbow. It might be a specific date, such as, "When the cast comes off your leg, you're not going to be running around immediately. People are usually disappointed at first. But two or three months after the cast comes off, you'll be feeling as good as new." That's the date you have to focus on, confident in the knowledge that it will happen eventually.

Sometimes doctors talk about the endpoint not in terms of a date but in terms of a process. Your doctor might say, "We have to give the medicine time to work, and that varies with people. Then we have to work at getting you the right diet and exercise program. But we'll figure it all out and then you'll be feeling much, much better."

It's good to know what the process is going to look like, but this still may not answer your question about an endpoint. So push a little. Ask something like this: "Okay, but are we talking more like two weeks, or five years? Should I think days, or should I think months?" Many doctors hate to be pinned down, but people should be able to put you in the ballpark with a rough estimate.

Also ask about the course of your progress. It's not just that it might take you six months before you feel better (that's okay—at least now you know where the boundary is), but within the six months, your path might not be straight up. Maybe you'll be feeling better and better while you're lying in bed, but when you get out of bed and start moving around, you might initially feel worse again. But if you know what to expect and understand that it's part of your six-month journey to recovery, it won't bother you as much.

What if you're told that your problem won't go away? Of course this is bad news, but the stress/discouragement response hears things in a slightly different way. It hears the hope that's contained in your knowing what you're up against. And it deals with this by saying, "Well, that's not the news I was hoping for, but now that I know what to expect, I can focus on symptom management and on picking up other tools for dealing with this problem. I don't have to waste emotional energy suffering from uncertainty."

"How bad will it get?" Most of us do something stupid when it comes to thinking about how bad our discomfort will get. We listen to our ignorant selves, and we tell ourselves some scary things. But we're afraid to ask someone who knows what she's talking about for the real scoop. Of course, we're afraid we'll learn something even worse than we've imagined. But if we remember that the main cause of the second illness is a sense of helplessness, that should change the way we approach this.

Nothing makes us feel more helpless than uncertainty. People can deal with bad news as long as it's clear, because then they'll figure out a way to cope. So if you can find out how bad your discomfort will get, then even if that's not good news, you'll have a better sense of how to cope, there will be less uncertainty, you'll have more of a sense of control, and your second illness will diminish.

Don't be afraid to ask these three questions. Even if you don't get the answers you were hoping for, you will probably get more than what you have now and you will definitely get greater clarity. And it's the clarity that puts boundaries around your fears and gives you hope. Plus the very act of asking will make you feel proactive. This, too, will make you feel more in control.

FINDING HOPE

The second illness blinds you to the reality that there are more reasons to hope than you can see right now, but to find these reasons to hope you have to look for them. This might sound obvious, but it needs saying when you're sick or injured, because when your body is under stress, you're not thinking as clearly as you usually do.

Hope's a funny thing. When you understand how it really works, it changes how you approach life. Hope, that little flame burning deep within you, actually works like an understanding boyfriend or girlfriend. Hope doesn't need to see you always delivering the goods. That's too much to expect. Hope just needs to see you trying. If you do your best, the flame of hope grows. Hope is a cheap date.

So the little flame of hope inside you is saying to you, "I don't know if you can make the pain go away [or stop the dizziness or the tremors, or ease the itchiness, or whatever], but I'll sure be happy if you look for help. Just look—that's all I'm asking."

So that's the deal between you and the hope within you.

You need to become as active as you can at looking for relief from your symptoms. Then your hope will grow. *And that's because your hope will know that you're not helpless, that in fact you've got real power.*

So, don't put up with symptoms that make you uncomfortable or constrict your life. If I had to devise one mantra for everyone who is sick or injured it would be, *"Solutions are out there."* And if you act as if solutions really are out there and keep looking no matter what, you will cure your second illness, no matter what else is going on with your body.

Now you may be saying to yourself, "How do I do that? I'm already doing the best I can. What more do you want from me?"

You're right about that. I'm sure you are doing the best you can. Certainly no one sits around saying that there's a lot more they could do to feel better, but they just don't want to do it. How, then, is it possible to do more when you think you can't do more?

It's very possible. I see people all the time who think they've "done everything," but they really haven't scratched the surface.

Mary, 34, for example, suffered from chronic lower back pain. This was particularly difficult for her because she taught fourth grade and she had to spend much of her day sitting, standing, bending. Mary was starting to get very discouraged, because the problem wouldn't go away and was causing her so much misery. She was also frightened that she might have to give up teaching at some point.

Mary was convinced that she'd done everything to help

herself. But it turns out that "everything" consisted solely of taking an ibuprofen every now and then and lying down as much as possible at home with her feet up. Now these may both be good things to do, but they're just the beginning of what can be done to help a painful lower back.

Mary's situation changed shortly after a new teacher was hired at her school in the middle of the year. They got to talking, and Mary mentioned her back problem. The woman said, "Oh I used to have the same problem, but it's all better now."

"You're lucky," Mary said. "I've got this really good recipe and I'm sticking to it, but it just hasn't worked yet."

"That's it?!" Then this woman told Mary all the different things she'd done. It was a vastly longer list. It included acupuncture, diet, special exercises, relaxation techniques, massage, and many more things. She couldn't say which of these had "worked." But she remembered clearly how empowered she'd felt trying different approaches. "You think you're trying," she said to Mary, "but if you don't mind my saying so, you've really just given up."

Ed, 22, got hit hard by infectious mononucleosis the summer he graduated from college. Now, of course Ed went to a good doctor and followed his recommendations. But week after week Ed continued to feel that he had no energy whatsoever. His mother suggested he see a nutritionist or a good practitioner of alternative medicine. "I'm not going to see one of those witch doctors," Ed said. "I just don't believe in that stuff, and nothing's going to make me change my mind."

Then Ed's mother told him that she'd felt the same way

when she had certain female problems. Her doctor, a believer in complementary medicine, had encouraged her to explore additional therapies. But she also "didn't believe in that stuff," as she'd put it to her doctor.

What her doctor said next surprised her. "You know," she said, "in all my years as a doctor I've learned that I've really got to be humble about what I have to offer. There's an awful lot we don't know. And we're learning new approaches all the time. Here's what I suggest. You don't have to believe in alternative approaches. Why would you? You don't know if they'll work for you. I don't either. But try them first. You may get relief for your discomfort from an unexpected source."

That was a new idea for Ed—trying something before you'd come to believe in it. It released Ed from being locked into an approach that wasn't helping him with his symptoms.

Simply believing that solutions are out there and actively searching for them won't guarantee you'll find a rapid cure for your physical problems. How can I say that? I don't know what your physical problems are! But believing and searching *will* cure the second illness. That's the enemy we're fighting here, you and I: anxiety, depression, and all the other miserable emotions that plague us when we get sick or injured.

The search for solutions sends a strong, clear signal to your emotional self that you're on the job taking care of yourself, and your emotional self responds by taking care of you. And then *you* feel better, whatever is going on with your body.

9

Facing Your Future with Confidence

We count on a future that doesn't yet exist to make us feel secure in the present. "I don't have a boyfriend right now, but I know that one day I'm going to be married." Or "I don't know what the hell is going on with my career, but one way or another I'm going to be able to retire one day and play all the golf I want." Or "I'm okay as long as I can look forward to watching my children grow up."

This is only natural. You can't wake up having absolutely no idea what the next day or next twenty years are going to bring. You have to have a sense of what you can expect. But if you count your chickens before they're hatched,

131

you're playing a dangerous game. It's great when the future you were counting on comes through for you, when you come down for breakfast and—*yes!*—you haven't run out of maple syrup so you *can* have those pancakes you were looking forward to. But when things don't turn out the way you'd hoped, and there's no syrup in that bottle you'd been noticing tucked away at the bottom of the fridge, you can be very disappointed.

It's much worse when you expect to go running and an injury takes that from you, or when you expect to have shapely breasts and an illness takes one of them from you. But let's remember the essence of the second illness. The stress/discouragement response is all about feeling helpless. Our expectations for the future make us feel strong and competent as long as they turn out the way we've hoped. If our expectations are dashed, there we are—feeling helpless.

People who deal with this successfully, though, have learned something valuable. Whenever we pin our hopes on one specific future, we're in trouble, because there are always so many ways things can go wrong. Why pin your entire happiness on one tiny little future coming true? So we've got to come up with ways of coming up with new futures for ourselves.

CREATING NEW OPTIONS

Donny loved tennis and running. But when he was in his forties, he noticed he was feeling a lot of pain on the bottom of his heels, the part you plant on the ground. It was starting to become such a problem that it often knocked him out of action. And when he woke up in the morning he had to walk gingerly because his heels were particularly tender then.

He told himself that it was probably nothing. But he couldn't lose the nagging suspicion that something was seriously wrong that would change his life. Donny was terrified. He didn't want to hear bad news. So he put off going to the doctor. When he finally went, he learned that because he'd been running around for years without proper cushioning in his shoes, the tendon that goes under the heel had gotten damaged beyond repair. Donny's time for playing tennis and going for runs was over.

That's when the second illness took over big time. Donny's sense of his future was destroyed. He was in despair. He saw himself getting fat and weak, and that there was nothing he could do about it. But the emotions we all have when we're dealing with illness or injury are like pigeons—there's never just one. When one emotion shows up, others will immediately join it. And in just this way fear followed despair for Donny.

He was terrified at the thought of what his future would be like. Then anger followed fear. He couldn't stop blaming himself for neglecting his feet. He blamed his wife for not making him go to the doctor. He blamed the doctor for not guessing that Donny might have this problem: "I run a lot, I'm not a kid, I'm carrying a few pounds—you do the math. What was wrong with that doctor?"

But Donny was lucky. Something happened that pulled him out of the stress/discouragement response. One of the guys at his company noticed Donny's downcast state and got concerned. Donny told him his story and the guy said, "So why don't you just try another form of exercise?"

"Yeah, I'd thought of that. But what can you do without your feet?"

"Well, think again, buddy," the guy said. "I had a similar problem. It was my knees. No more pounding it out for me either. Then I got into two great sports. Rowing and swimming. They both use your whole body. Very active. Very challenging. A lot of fun. But your feet and knees don't take a beating at all."

A whole new world opened up for Donny. The guy had been right. There were amazing possibilities out there. But Donny had gotten stuck because he'd stopped believing in those amazing possibilities. If you believe in them, you'll search for them. If you search for them, you'll find them.

It's amazing how much the emotional fallout from illness or injury has to do with your sense of what's going to happen in the future. No matter how sick you are, if God himself promised that you'd be all better *tomorrow* when you wake up, you'd instantly feel a heck of a lot better. Animals never fall victim to the second illness, mainly because the future is not a concept they carry around in their heads.

If you can learn to deal with the emotions you have about how your illness or injury is going to affect your future, you'll eliminate one of the major sources of the second illness.

YOU CAN ALWAYS FIND SOMETHING TO LOOK FORWARD TO

The antidote to helplessness is not necessarily control. Just as good is having a sense of options. And thank goodness, because while we can't control our future, it turns out that there are always options, no matter what. And so there's always hope, no matter what. And so there's always an antidote to our fear and despair about the future when we get sick or injured.

I can go even further. I can promise you that no matter how much you think your future has been changed, you can always find something to look forward to. Maybe your old future still awaits you—you've just taken a detour, and you need to find your way back. Maybe there's a new future filled with new possibilities you can't quite appreciate yet.

I've worked with patients who find themselves facing every future you can imagine, including all the futures we dread the most. And it's an incontrovertible fact that once people realistically accept that things have changed, it is *always* possible to find some hope in their new future.

An important element in the new future is the new you in that future. It may be a new you that gets tired more easily than you're used to. It may be a new you without a gall bladder. It may be a new you who can no longer play tennis. But a new self can be accommodated, if you approach the future with the expectation that there's something there for you.

People like Donny who've recovered from seeing a future dashed have all made a wonderful discovery. They've seen that they had an ability that they never thought they had: the ability to find new possible futures, to choose them, and to make them happen. This means you're never helpless.

There's always a future with something good in it, even if it's not the future you would have chosen for yourself. As long as you exercise your power and freedom to create a new future, you will feel better fast.

People can do this no matter what problem they are facing.

A person develops arthritis and realizes that physical activity will have to be limited. Okay. Maybe this is a great opportunity to learn a new language or to take singing lessons. Maybe you can even surprise yourself by muddling on. When the artist Renoir got serious arthritis in his hands later in his life, he had brushes strapped to his hands so he could paint.

If you happen to have a physical problem right now, I hope it's not serious. But I want to tell you about a woman who had the most serious problem any of us can imagine. You may feel her problem is nothing like yours, and it probably isn't. But my point is this: if *she* can find a way to give herself a new sense of a future and feel less helpless in the process, then we all can. And this eliminates our sense of fear.

Amanda's story. Amanda had everything to live for. A loving husband. Two bright young sons. And a sense that she was deeply needed by the people she loved.

Then she was told that her cervical cancer had become terminal. This is about the worst news most of us can imagine. How could anyone possibly find hope in this brief, barren new future?

At first it felt impossible. Amanda went through the stages dying people go through seemingly all at once: rage, despair, denial, bargaining, you name it. Only acceptance was missing. It felt like being punched in the stomach, except that the feeling went on for weeks.

And it was all about fear. Fear of what she was losing, of what her family was losing, of what her now-short future held in store for her.

Then it hit her—this emotional tailspin was as toxic as the cancer itself. She was sobbing as she said to me, "I know I'm going to die from this cancer. I don't have any choice about that. So the time I have left is all the more precious. And this is where I do have a choice. If I let myself go into an emotional tailspin, it will rob me of any possibility of joy in the time I have left. And who's to say that I can't find joy, or at least some kind of comfort or satisfaction in this time."

And so Amanda kept open the possibility that she'd find something that would give her hope. Then one day she was thinking about her children growing up without her. Somehow by luck or inspiration or the grace of God, she started thinking about what she could give them to make their future better, and she had the idea of making a series of video letters. Maybe there *would* be a way for her to be in their lives as they were growing up.

This was a big project and it took creativity and strength,

but because it was all about hope, it gave her far more joy than it took from her. Her plan was to make one video letter, maybe only ten minutes each, for each birthday for each son up until the age of 21. And that wasn't all. She'd also make a video letter for all the big landmarks in each of their lives—graduation, marriage, first child, and so on. She'd tell them how proud she was of them. She'd talk about the good qualities each of them had. She'd give them some motherly advice. She'd talk about her own experiences at their age. She'd tell them again how much she loved them.

Once she started she suddenly realized, "What about my husband? What is he, chopped liver?" So she also made as many video letters for him as she could, to be sent to him each year on their anniversary.

The hope lay in how much better Amanda could make things and in how many gifts she could give. They were not the gifts she'd wanted to give her kids—her presence as they were growing up—but they were real gifts nonetheless. And here's the key. New hope is always possible because there's always something hopeful you can find to do. Even if it wasn't your first choice, the fact that you're choosing it and doing it will give you comfort and hope, and this will help cure your second illness.

Knowing you can do this is how to lay to rest your fears of the future. You don't need to make everything all better to cure the second illness. Amanda demonstrates that anyone can find hope no matter what their future, and if you find the hope and act on it, you will feel better emotionally.

The second illness won't get the better of you as long as

you realize that you always have choices. In fact, you have more choices now that you're taking a creative stance towards your future than you did when you counted on one simple future. And best of all, you have the power to make the new future you choose *happen*.

LETTING GO OF YOUR OLD FUTURE

What about the future you've lost? Almost every illness or injury, let's face it, does mean losing some piece of the future you've planned on, even if it's only missing out on fun because you have to stay home all weekend with a cold. But if all you have in your head is your lost weekend, you'll never be able to think about anything else. Saying *no* to something in your mind will never make it go away. A painful thought is like a two-year old who wants to play with your telephone. The only thing that will work is distraction. You have to entice him with something more entertaining.

It's the same way when it comes to obsessing over a future we've lost. You will let go of it but only when you distract yourself by enticing yourself with something that's also worth looking forward to. This works no matter how big the loss is. Amanda could only begin to accept her death when she found a project that would help her live on in her family's life, and this gave her a future she could think about.

So here's the drill. You're sick or injured. You have fears about your future. Most of your fears have to do with some sort of threatened loss, from a lost weekend to a lost life. If the loss is real, the fear is real. But you're not helpless, and so there's always something you can give yourself that will in some small way substitute for what you've lost. Focus on that. And your sense of loss will evaporate.

10
Eight Steps to Living Without Anxiety

Often fear and anxiety create the most damaging emotional fallout that someone who's sick or injured has to deal with. Sometimes we're afraid of what lies in the future. Sometimes we're afraid of what's happening right now. Sometimes we have no idea why we're afraid. Whatever the cause, fear acts like a giant that scoops you up and grabs you in his huge, cold, clammy hands. You feel utterly paralyzed.

It's at a time like this when it's most important to show yourself that you're not helpless, not at all. I'm about to give you a technique that enables men and women just like you to turn the giant of fear into an irrelevant pipsqueak.

This technique is based on a simple but well proven idea: feelings follow thoughts, not the other way around. You don't think the lion is going to eat you because you're afraid of him. You're afraid of the lion because you think he's going to eat you. If you're filled with an upsetting emotion, it comes from the thoughts that have popped into your head, from whatever you happen to be telling yourself in the moment.

For example, you're at the doctor's office, you see the needle, and you burst out into a cold sweat of fear. But your fear actually comes from a real thought, from words that are zipping through your head: "That needle is going to cause me real pain." Now if you tell yourself, "Don't be afraid," that won't work at all. But if you change the thought and instead tell yourself something like, "It will just be a little pinch," then your feelings will change. It's hard to feel afraid when all you're anticipating is something you know doesn't hurt much at all.

Every anxiety is the product of specific thoughts. They might be big, vague thoughts that don't stand up to close examination: "I'm doomed." They might be wildly exaggerated thoughts: "I'll never get better." They might be incorrect thoughts: "This medicine isn't working."

You look for the thoughts that cause the feeling because you can change those thoughts and that will reverse the feeling. That is how it works, and I'll show you how it can work for you.

Maybe something suddenly terrifies you. "What's that lump!" Or, "What if I can never go jogging again!" Or, "I could die during that operation!" Maybe your fear isn't so sudden, more a nagging obsessive worry: "Yeah, I'm better now, but I keep being afraid I'm going to get sick again."

Here's the procedure for lessening your fear.

You'll learn to ask yourself eight questions whenever you're afraid. All these questions came from my research into what people do who successfully resist the fears that plague the rest of us. When you do what they did, it will work for you, too.

If you find that you're feeling anxious in connection with a health problem, ask yourself each one of these questions, and try to come up with the most honest answer that you can think of.

When you see what your answers are in the cold light of day, two things will happen. You'll have a chance to see if your answers make sense or not. And if you realize that they don't make sense, you'll have a chance to come up with answers that do make sense to you.

As you ask yourself each question and come up with your own answers, you'll find that your fear will dwindle down to almost nothing.

1. ASK YOURSELF
What am I actually afraid of?

Sometimes we know what makes us afraid, but lots of times we don't. Maybe you're suffering from a condition that leaves you feeling weak and tired. All you know is . . . you're afraid. But you probably haven't taken the time and trouble to identify exactly what you're scared of. It's the big, sloppy, overgeneralized fears that are most toxic and least realistic.

Identify exactly what it is that you're afraid of. Make a list if you need to. Then take them one at a time. "I'm afraid I won't be able to work." "I'm afraid it will just get worse." "I'm afraid that my spouse will get disgusted with me." "I'm afraid my doctor doesn't know what he's doing."

The moment people identify exactly what they're afraid of, they feel less afraid. What they're afraid of turns out to be specific and that makes it feel more manageable than the nameless dread they'd been dealing with. And once you've identified exactly what you're afraid of, you'll be in a position to answer the following questions, which will continue to reduce your fear.

2. ASK YOURSELF
Is this actually something I should be afraid of?

Do you remember when you were a kid and there'd be a branch outside scraping on your window or the shadow of a toy looming on your ceiling, and you'd be terrified by what you imagined it was? Then your mom or dad would come in, turn on the light, and show you what was really going on, and you'd realize there was nothing to be scared of.

We can do this for ourselves when we're grownups. Once we see what the thought in our head is that's scaring us, we can check out whether what we're afraid of is really something we should be afraid of.

And just the way you needed your mom and dad when you were a kid, you need someone with expertise now that you're an adult.

Here's what I do to see if what's going on is something I really need to be afraid of: I check in with people who should know. I used to be afraid of flying, for example. One of the techniques I learned to help me deal with my fear is what I call the "I'll panic when you tell me to" technique. This is pretty simple. The plane is bouncing around or swooping at an uncomfortable angle, and I'll look at the flight attendants or at passengers who seem like they fly a lot. If these people are calmly going about their business, hey, why should I push the panic button?

These people function as my personal panic panel. I'm uncomfortable asking them directly for reassurance. But I get all the reassurance I need by watching them.

We all need panic panels in our lives, never more so than when we're sick or injured. And fortunately most of us have people we can talk to—family, friends, and professionals. It's important that we do so, rather than keeping quiet out of fear of panicking them. You see, here's the secret. When you ask someone for reassurance, they may be scared, too, but by giving you reassurance, they'll have an opportunity to calm their own fears.

Your panic panel can reassure you no matter what your concerns. Maybe you're afraid of an unsightly scar following shoulder surgery. Or maybe you're afraid of living with a colostomy bag. Maybe you're afraid of losing your hearing, or your sight. Maybe you're afraid of losing a body part—a uterus or a testicle, a leg or a breast, one of your kidneys. Whatever your fear, you can tell yourself, "I don't need to panic until my panic panel panics." And if you're still not sure, *ask* them if this is something for you to be concerned about.

3. ASK YOURSELF
What's the worst that can happen?

There's simply no point in being afraid if, once you've looked into it, the worst that can happen isn't really something so terrible. Just because you're dealing with an illness or injury doesn't mean that in your particular case the worst probable outcome is all that big a deal.

Artie, 37, thought he was way too young to have an ulcer. But he really hit the panic button when he started thinking that he'd never again be able to eat most of his favorite foods. This was very discouraging for him. But he had failed to check out what the worst probable outcome was. It turns out that with the terrific medicine available, given his condition, there were many foods he had to avoid *but only temporarily*. It was overwhelmingly likely that his ulcer would heal and then, with a little moderation, he could go back to eating what he enjoyed.

It's amazing how many fears go away when you discover that the worst that can happen in your particular case is probably not such a big deal.

But what if the worst that could happen *is* a big deal?

4. ASK YOURSELF
How likely is it?

Maybe one of your fears is that you'll die from whatever is wrong with you. And maybe, as it turns out, you have an illness where the worst thing that could happen really is that you just might die. And maybe you're in so much discomfort that you feel you're going to die at any moment. But then again, it may be that once you check it out, you'll find that death is a unlikely outcome. You deserve the relief from anxiety that comes from seeing that what you're afraid of is pretty unlikely to happen.

And don't let doctors scare you when they tell you that there is "some risk of death" from some procedure you're about to go through. They may have to say that. You should ask what that risk actually is. Fifty/fifty? Yikes! But it's almost certainly *not* that high. It's probably more like one in 6,000 (wait a minute: that's your probability of dying in a traffic accident *this year*) or one in 200 (which is pretty high, but it's still something like the probability you'll die in a traffic accident over the course of your entire lifetime). And yet you drive all the time without a thought.

Still scared? You shouldn't be. Most fears are quickly forgotten when you take a close look at how unlikely they are to come true.

People are always going nuts about the scary disease of the month. But the probability of contracting SARS, Avian flu, or whatever is low and the probability of dying from them is even lower. Most of these highly publicized exotic diseases are less lethal than influenza, which people get every day.

No matter what it is you're afraid of, don't confuse panic with information. Your panic is not information about the real odds you face. Learn what the real odds are and love the odds, because they're probably in your favor. Most of the things you're afraid of will lose their power to scare you when you realize how unlikely they are ever to happen.

At least they're much more unlikely than you think right now. A 19-year-old woman got into a car crash. She thought she was fine at first, but almost immediately her neck started hurting her more and more. No matter what position she'd be in, she'd soon start getting neck pain. The whole thing was quite literally a huge pain in the neck! She made the rounds of chiropractors, massage therapists, internists, acupuncturists, and specialists in spinal-cord injuries. Every imaginable test was performed. People had theories, but there was no clear sense of what the problem was, and certainly no one had any cure for her. She went right to the catastrophe: "I'll never get better." (Which was really her way of saying, "It's 100 percent likely that I'll never get better.")

"Really?" I asked her. "Never? All kinds of things can happen. Time itself might heal what's bothering you. That happens all the time. New diagnostic tools appear. New treatments come up all the time. There may be someone out there right now who's successfully treating people with your problem and you just haven't hooked up with him. Why don't you figure out as many ways as you can how this problem in your neck can be solved. The more ways you come up with, the more likely it is you'll get better."

And she did just that. In fact she came up with over a

dozen ways a cure might be right around the corner. The point is that no matter what's scaring you, it's probably less likely than you think, and you can usually come up with ways to make that outcome even less likely. And that's where you should be devoting your thoughts.

As you continue answering these questions, notice how your fear continues to get smaller and weaker.

5. ASK YOURSELF
Can I prevent this?

You remember the basic principle for curing the second illness. Whenever you act less helpless and more proactive, you'll heal the negative emotions that come with your primary illness or injury. You don't have to actually move mountains to accomplish this. You just need to feel you have a chance to be effective.

So there you are, dealing with some condition, and you have specific fears for the future. You know what the worst thing that can happen is, and you know how likely it is, and, frankly, you're not all that reassured. So look for ways you can prevent the worst thing that can happen. If you can find something that will give you that ounce of protection, you have a chance to enormously increase the odds in your favor. A little protective action can mean a great lowering of risk and a lot less anxiety for you.

Take Joan, who was diagnosed with adult-onset diabetes when she was in her thirties. She was scared, because she knew there was a risk that as she got older more medical problems could hit her. She foresaw a downward slide ahead physically and fell into a depression that lasted for months. It got so bad that it almost cost her both her job and her marriage. This was a classic example of the second illness at its worst.

"What's wrong with you?" people kept saying to her impatiently, the way they often do to someone who's suffering from the second illness. Joan wasn't able to bring herself to say the words, "I'm falling apart and there's nothing I can do about it," but that was how she felt.

Joan was lucky enough to have a doctor who understood the emotional impact of her condition. He told her to take the energy she spent thinking about her risks and put it towards coming up with ways to lower those risks. If she did this, she'd almost certainly live a long, healthy life and would definitely pull herself out of her emotional tailspin.

Joan followed his instructions. She discovered that for every legitimate risk (like, say, losing a toe or foot because of circulatory problems) there were indeed specific effective steps she could take to drastically diminish that risk. Of course, the future stayed unknown, as it always does for all of us. But because Joan had preventive steps she could take, and because she took them, her sense of effectiveness went up and her depression went away.

6. ASK YOURSELF
Can I do something so I don't feel alone with what I'm going through?

Fear recedes mightily when you feel you're not alone. One woman walking by herself down a dark street at night might feel scared. Two women walking together will feel a lot less scared. Three women walking together might not feel scared at all.

If you're not talking to people who have wise or comforting ways of responding about what you're going through, then you have to start talking to them now. Many of us get very private when it comes to an illness or injury. And that hurts you.

The more people you have in your life you can turn to for support, the faster you'll recover from the second illness and the better you'll feel overall. Look around—you probably have these people in your life already. It's your willingness to turn to them that makes all the difference.

How exactly do you find people who can be supportive? They're everywhere—at your office, your church, your club, in your neighborhood, maybe sitting next to you in your doctor's office. Maybe there are support groups for people going through what you're going through.

Be confident that people will be happy to talk to you and offer you reassurance. They'll be flattered you've asked them for help. They'll be relieved to know that your life turns out to be as imperfect as their own life is. (Everyone thinks that the other guy has it more together than they do.) And they'll be pleased to find themselves in the role of expert and confidant.

What's the worst that can happen? That when you need someone the most, they won't be there for you? There are people in our lives like that. All I can say is that it's better to find out who they are sooner rather than later.

It's important to ask for reassurance directly: "I'm going

through blah, blah, blah and I'm afraid of yadda, yadda, yadda. I really need some reassurance here." You have to ask for reassurance, because if you don't, and you just say, "I'm afraid of blah, blah, blah," the other person might say, "Yeah, I'm afraid of blah, blah, blah, too." And then what have you got?

Don't forget to ask people what they've learned from their own experiences. This will save you from making the same mistakes they did. A good question to ask is, "What do you wish you'd done differently when you were going through this?"

7. ASK YOURSELF
Can I insure myself against this?

I'm not talking about the kind of insurance you buy. I'm talking about doing something so that if the thing you're afraid of happens, you'll still be okay or at least have some compensation. We use this broader concept of insurance in our lives all the time. It's why you take an umbrella to work when you hear there might be rain later in the afternoon.

All you have to do is think about things you can do to take care of yourself just in case what you're afraid of comes to pass.

Let's say you're scheduled for open-heart surgery. There's a small risk you won't make it through, and that's what you're afraid of. So you need insurance in case the worst happens. Insurance here lies in doing things to take care of yourself and your family. Do you have a will? Have you written long letters to all the people you love in your life telling them how much they matter to you and how much you've gotten from them, and apologizing for all the ways you've hurt them? Have you gotten your financial affairs in order?

Now you might say, so what, I'd still be dead. But from the point of view of healing your emotional state, these precautions attack anxiety the way an antibiotic attacks infection. Doing something rather than nothing is what makes all the difference. And there are always things we can do to give ourselves some insurance, no matter what we're afraid of.

One final question brings your fear down to the lowest possible level.

8. ASK YOURSELF
What could I do to cope if what I'm afraid of happened?

People often overlook this question when they get caught up in fear. They get so panicky that they fail to realize that if the thing they're afraid of happened, they would actually be able to cope rather well.

Patricia had always dreamed of having children one day. But she put off getting pregnant until she and her husband were more established in their careers and able to afford a nice house. Just when she started trying to get pregnant, she started having problems with pain and bleeding, and her doctor told her she needed a hysterectomy. She was stunned. But second and third opinions confirmed that this was necessary.

Patricia ended up in a state of tremendous rage and anxiety. She was impossible to live with, and she found it impossible to live with herself. She was sure that not being able to have children of her own would be a disaster she'd never recover from. Of course she knew she could adopt, but she was convinced that would not be the same at all.

Then Patricia met a woman at a neighborhood barbecue—this woman had recently moved there. They got to talking, and Patricia learned that this woman had been adopted, and when she and her husband couldn't conceive, they ended up adopting two children.

She said to Patricia, "As someone who was adopted myself, almost the only thing I ever wanted was biological children of my own. I almost convinced myself that I couldn't live unless I got that. But you know, we so often take these positions and lock ourselves into them emotionally. We make ourselves think we're more fragile than we really are, like we'll break if we don't get what we want. But once I let myself live with the possibility of adopting, it was like a light went on. I saw I'd be okay with it."

Patricia asked her so many questions about adoption that she was afraid she was starting to be rude. But a light started to come on for Patricia. Her basic assumption that she wouldn't be able to cope if she couldn't give birth started crumbling. She saw a glimpse of the opposite, that she'd be able to cope beautifully. This woman had. And why should Patricia think this woman was any stronger than she was?

And this is something we all need to do when we're faced with a fear that panics us. Without realizing it, we have a thought in our heads that says, "Of course I won't be able to cope." Who wouldn't panic in the face of a thought like that?

But suppose we held in our heads the opposite. Suppose we thought, "Of course I *will* be able to cope." That wonderful thought becomes like a railroad engine pulling a train of thoughts behind it, and they're all thoughts about specific ways we would be able to cope. And that can have a huge effect on your inner emotional climate.

Assume the best about your ability to cope, not the worst, because most people can actually cope much better than they think they can.

Let's get started. Make a list of things you could do to cope if whatever you're afraid of happened. Just write down the first ideas that come into your head. Maybe this list doesn't look like much *yet*. But you're just getting started. Up until now, you've put your energy into being afraid—no wonder you don't have a lot of ideas *yet* for how you'd cope. But if you put some of that energy into brainstorming new ways to cope, your list will grow longer and better. Then the very fact that you can make a list like this will make you feel much less helpless.

Here's another tool to show yourself that you can cope. Every time scary, negative thoughts come into your head, say these words to yourself: "Be constructive." I'm not asking you to say, "Be positive." That's not how you feel. I'm just asking you to use this scary moment as an opportunity to think of specific things you can do that would help.

Feel Better Fast

Fear is just a form of energy. You can use that energy to paralyze yourself or you can use that energy more constructively to think of new options. Maybe you won't come up with any great new options right away. But that's okay. It's putting your energy into looking for constructive options that will relieve your anxiety.

These eight questions amount to a simple, tested, and powerful program for eliminating your burden of fear about the future. Yes, it would be even simpler to take a pill. But a pill isn't going to change the way you think about things. When you get sick or injured, you don't have anxiety because some chemical in your brain has suddenly gotten out of whack. You have anxiety because you're suddenly faced with very real challenges, and all the pills in the world won't give you the inner resources necessary to feel that you can cope with these challenges.

Asking these questions, pursuing the search for good answers, and then focusing on the good answers you come up with is something you can do. Or, if you want, you can just continue to suffer. At least now you have a choice.

11

How to Increase Your Emotional Energy

"**I** feel like my nerves have been rubbed raw." "I feel like I'm running on empty, like I'm depleted down to my very core." "I don't know if I feel more blue or blah—I feel so down and flat."

These are people describing the way illness or injury can be a blow to our emotional energy.

But the emotional-energy story is actually a good-news story for people who are sick or injured. It offers a back-door way to recapture much or all of what you've lost through your body. It's like going to a casino, losing a lot of money, asking for it back, and having some little man come up to you and say, "Well, if you really want your money back, just go to room 107 and ask for Fred." And guess what? You go to room 107 and Fred does give you your money back.

You can't do that at any casino I've ever heard of, but you can do it when it comes to the energy you lose when you get sick or injured.

Let's define our terms. We all know what physical energy is. It's what you run low on when you're not fed enough sources of physical energy like sleep, healthful food, and exercise. Physical energy is also what takes a hit when something goes wrong with your body. Even a cold leaves you weak. I know a guy who badly tore a ligament in his ankle, and with the pain, the rehab, the surgery, and the various casts he had to wear, he was so physically exhausted that it jeopardized his already shaky marriage. And there are plenty of illnesses—hypothyroidism is but one example—that directly attack your physical energy.

Your total energy is defined as your ability to be up for your life. This includes your willingness to take on tasks, your tolerance for frustration, your ability to keep going. But your total energy doesn't just come from your physical energy. The other ingredient in your total energy is your emotional energy. *Over 70 percent of your total energy comes from your emotional energy*. That's how important emotional energy is.

Think of it like this. You were up until two o'clock in the morning cleaning out your closets, because the next day they were going to take away the dumpster you'd rented. Now, a mere four hours later, the alarm goes off. It's six in the morning! You have no more desire to get up than you have to stick an ice pick in your forehead. You are, you think, completely exhausted.

But then you remember . . . your best friend is coming in an hour to pick you up for a road trip you've been planning for months. Psyched! Suddenly you feel up for the day, and you bounce out of bed.

Now notice: you're just as physically tired as you were a moment ago. But the thought of this exciting trip with your friend fills you full of energy. *This extra energy is all coming from your emotional energy._*

So you can have almost all the energy you're looking for if you have enough emotional energy. That's great news, but the great news doesn't stop there. There are things you can do to *give* yourself all the emotional energy you need. In fact, there are so many sources of emotional energy that you can be up for life no matter how bad things are for you physically.

You don't think so? Then how is it that some people *on their deathbeds* make jokes, promote acts of healing among family members, reassure their loved ones, and have plenty of hope for what is to come? You have to be thinking that, physically, they're feeling rather poorly! But this is a sign of how powerful emotional energy is.

The most important thing for you to know about emotional energy is that it's entirely within your power to increase it, no matter who you are, no matter what you're dealing with. The next most important thing for you to know is that if you're struggling with the second illness, you *need* to boost your emotional energy to help you deal with the mental and emotional fallout from your injury or illness.

So what do you do? Here are some tips from my research that are especially important for people dealing with a physical problem.

Understand that your life now is all about your emotional energy. So do an emotional energy audit. What gives you emotional energy? What drains it? The simplest way to do this is to think about everything in your life, everything you do, every person you interact with, *everything*, and ask if it makes you feel up or down.

For example, think about the very last thing you did. Maybe it was taking your dog for a walk. Maybe it was getting your kids on to the school bus. Maybe it was talking on the phone to your boss. Did that activity leave you feeling more positive? More happy? More calm? More focused? More satisfied? If so, then it was a source of emotional energy. That means it's something you should have more of in your life.

But maybe what you did left you feeling glum in a way you can't quite put your finger on. Maybe in some way it raised your anxiety level. Maybe it left you feeling badly about yourself. Maybe it just made you want to lie down. If so, then it was something that drained your emotional energy, and it's something you need less of in your life.

There are, of course, many things about our lives that we can't change. But if you know that you can add emotional energy boosters to your life and subtract energy drainers, then you have a sense of control. And as I've shown, you will feel better fast whenever you increase your sense that you have control in your life. This doubles your emotional energy. You get emotional energy from what you do to increase it, and you get it from knowing *that you can* do things to increase it. Wow!

Concentrate on what you can do, not on what you can't do. When something goes wrong with our bodies, our lives shrink, even if only a little. Let's say you're chopping vegetables in the kitchen and cut your thumb. It's nothing really. You clean the wound, put a bandage on, and you're all set. And yet you suddenly find that it's awkward doing things that you took for granted a minute before. Your world has shrunk.

It's easy to see how when you're laid low by something serious, you can spend your days like the little match girl, peering through the window at all the happy, warm people making merry in ways she never can.

But if you think about the fact that you can always increase your emotional energy, you'll be in a position to answer these questions: What are the opportunities my illness or injury has made possible for me? What are things I can do now that I wasn't able to do before?

At first maybe nothing will come to you, but soon you'll realize that the opportunities are endless. Maybe there are books you can finally get to read now. Maybe there are people in your life you can get closer to. Maybe there are decisions you can get clear about. Maybe you can deepen your spirituality. Heck, maybe this is your chance to get people to finally sympathize with you a little bit.

Don't stop until you've come up with ten new opportunities your illness or injury has now made possible for you.

Avoid stressful situations. Most of us today are like waiters in a busy restaurant: we can only carry so many plates of stress at a time. And most of us are carrying more than our share already. Then along comes some health problem, and that's a big platter of stress all by itself. This means that to *increase* your emotional energy you have to *decrease* the parts of your life that give you stress.

You can eliminate stress in big ways and little. Leave extra early for a doctor's appointment, for example. Sure it's a bummer to sit there in a waiting room. But you can always read a good book! But by leaving early you'll eliminate the stress that comes from being afraid that you'll be late for your appointment and maybe even lose it.

Generally, do whatever you do in the least stressful way. Let's say you want to have a meal. Maybe the least stressful way is to pick up some takeout. Maybe the least stressful way is to tell everyone to get out of your kitchen so you can prepare the food without anyone being in your way. Maybe the least stressful way is to open a can. And if there's a least stressful way to have a meal, there's a least stressful way to do *anything*.

Try to eliminate stressful people from your life. Maybe, for example, you have a cousin who's always bugging you to try weird remedies for your malady, and you find this as annoying as hell. Don't talk to this cousin! You don't need the stress.

Or at least prevent the people in your life from stressing

you out. People who are sick or injured tell me that for some reason there are people that are close to them who love them but who also, somehow, bug them a lot. They can do it in little ways, like always asking how you're feeling. They can do it by never seeming to be aware of how you're feeling. Well, don't assume these people are evil, even if they seem evil sometimes. Instead, assume that they're acting clueless or insensitive because they quite literally don't know how to act better. Tell these people ways you want to be treated that will give you the least stress.

And help them help you. Even if it seems like they're being willfully stupid or "passive aggressive," it's much more likely that they're simply on a learning curve. So if you say, "I need you to not make any demands on me for the next period," and five minutes later they come in and ask you where the spatula is, they may not realize that asking you questions is also making demands on you.

People also tell me that no matter how badly off they are physically, even if they're in intensive care, as long as they're conscious there will still be people in their lives who will make demands on them. I know one guy, for example, who was recovering from a triple bypass, and things weren't going all that well. His wife asked him if he would be willing to see her second cousin, Herbie, who was waiting outside, "because Herbie came such a long way"! Well, if you want to minimize stress, "Just say no." In general, before you say yes to any request, however small it seems, however important someone tries to make it, ask yourself how stressful it will be for you to follow through. If you see stress ahead, don't do it.

Learn how to stop worrying. Worry is a tumor on your emotional energy. It eats away at it until there's nothing left.

But wait a minute, you might say. I have real problems here. How can I avoid worrying?

We can't avoid problems in life, but we *can* avoid worry. What is worry anyway? Worry is just a very bad way of thinking about problems. Think about the last time you were worrying about something. I know just what you were doing. You were thinking about how *big* your problem was, exploring all the dimensions of its bigness. You were thinking about how *bad* your problem was, delving into all the depths of its badness. We know this is true, because after we've worried about a problem we always come away impressed with the sheer problem-ness of the problem.

Well, if worry is a bad way of dealing with a problem, there are plenty of good ways.

Remember that you've been a problem solver all your life. So the key is *to do something* when a problem comes into your mind. Do anything, no matter what, as fast as possible. You don't have to solve a problem to kill a worry. The part of you that's prone to worry is just afraid that you're not going to show up for yourself. As long as you act, as long as you do something rather than nothing, the worry part of you will relax. The more you act, the less likely you are to worry because now your mind trusts you to take care of your life. You don't have to do something great, you just have to do *something*.

Another thing to do instead of worrying is *talk to someone smart*. Notice I didn't say talk to someone who will listen to you. Maybe you'll feel better if someone just listens, but you'll feel *a lot* better if the person you're talking to is in the position of making some halfway intelligent suggestions.

And another good thing to do is try what I call *anti-worrying*. This may sound like a new idea, but I bet that in some way you've been doing it all your life. Worrying is thinking about how things are not going to be okay. Anti-worrying is thinking about how things *will* be okay. It takes the same amount of brain energy to anti-worry as it docs to worry, but it makes you feel sooooo much better.

You may be a little rusty. Let's say you hurt your back. Suddenly you're worried about how you're going to do your job, what's going to happen to your social life, and so on. Now, even though it might feel a little awkward at first, try anti-worrying. How, for example, will things on your job be okay? Maybe you can get some time off. Maybe some pain killers will make things bearable. Maybe you'll get a lot of sympathy from moaning around the office. Maybe it will mend faster than you'd thought.

And how will your social life be okay? Anti-worrying allows you to focus on the nice long phone calls you can have with your friends instead of going out. Anti-worrying makes you think about someone you're interested in maybe coming over and taking care of you a little bit, so that the two of you get closer.

We need to get out of the trap of thinking that worrying is inevitable. It's not. It's just a kind of thinking. It takes absolutely no more effort to think about how things will be okay, and this anti-worrying will do wonders for your emotional energy.

As a last resort, after you've tried anti-worrying, after you've taken positive actions to deal with your problem, then you're in a position to try to let yourself live in the moment. You can do this because you've already taken care of business. All that's left is the moment. Pay attention to the sights and sounds and sensations of right now. If a worry floats into your head, say to yourself, "That's the future. Right now. . . ," and focus on the present moment.

Take care of the basics. Your overall energy level, physical as well as emotional, rests on a foundation of getting enough sleep, regular exercise, and a healthy diet. All of these can fall by the wayside when you get sick or injured.

Don't neglect the basics. If anything is hindering your ability to sleep, deal with it. For example, talk to your doctor about any prescriptions you may be taking that could be keeping you up. Maybe this is a time when medication to help you sleep would be very helpful. You may want to monitor how much you're sleeping during the day—maybe fewer or shorter naps would make it easier for you to sleep more at night. Try spending as little time in bed during the day as possible. Even just spending the day on the sofa instead of in bed will help you sleep when you go to bed.

Exercise can also make it easier for you to sleep at night. But exercise also has a lot of other benefits. You will feel better about yourself and you will recover faster. Of course your exercise should be within the limits of your ability, and you should always check with your doctor about how much exercise is appropriate for you. Even if you're so under the weather that you don't feel like moving, getting up to get things for yourself from the kitchen might actually prove to be a beneficial form of exercise. If you can't use your legs, exercise your arms. If nothing else, spend a few minutes several times a day tensing and relaxing as many muscles in your body as you can.

It's never been more important to eat well than now. When we're sick or injured, we too often eat too many of the wrong kinds of food, either because we want to indulge ourselves or because it's hard for us to prepare more healthful foods. This is a big mistake. It might seem like a cosmic injustice to go on a health diet just when you're feeling poorly, but what's more likely to make you feel better? In many ways, healthy food is the best medicine. And when it comes to healing the second illness, it will have great emotional benefits for you to know that you're doing everything possible to eat well.

12

Getting the Most out of Your Support System

When you get sick or injured, you can no longer be there for the people in your life the way you used to. Now you need them to be there for you. But too often the people we're counting on most to take care of us drop the ball. Too often we get frustrated with them.

When this happens, the stress and discouragement that come from not feeling cared for can give us a bad case of the second illness. This is too bad, because these same people, in most cases, can actually do a great job of coming through for us. We just have to learn how to do a better job of eliciting the help we need from them.

BEYOND THE FAIRY TALE

I understand what it's like to be laid up. I've been there myself when I had my heart attack and at other times, and I've talked to many people who've told me in depth what this experience is like. You feel helpless, because you are helpless to one degree or another. And the people around you, no matter how sensitive and caring they are, don't fully grasp what you're going through—your pain, your fear, your sense of isolation, your long uncomfortable nights and boring days. And what happened to all those people who love you? Suddenly they're impatient, distracted, and insensitive.

If you feel let down by those who should make up your support system, take comfort. This is very common.

Amy went through a period where she started having bad headaches, and her vision was impaired. She was already slightly hypocondriacal, but her fear of a brain tumor, or God knows what else, pushed all her buttons. Understandably, she needed her fiancé to "be there for her," but she made Jerry's life a living hell. She wanted to talk about her condition all the time, always complaining, always assuming the worst. Whenever he tried to reassure her, she attacked him for dismissing her concerns. She asked him to do a hundred and one little things for her, but her needs tumbled forth so rapidly that Jerry never knew whether to respond to the first thing she said, the last thing, or what. It didn't matter, because whatever he did for her was the wrong thing done in the wrong way.

The truth is that Amy was terrified and in pain. But Jerry felt that he was being made to jump through hoops while getting whipped in the process. He got so sick of Amy, that they had huge fights, and in the end they actually broke up over this.

This is not a rare story. Many relationships are damaged as a result of what happens when someone is sick or injured.

But the damage isn't always to the relationship. Sometimes the same strains that could hurt the relationship hurt the patient instead. Tony knew that his wife, Shana, was very busy with her job, their kids, her family, so he didn't want to ask for what he needed when he came home from hernia surgery. He actually needed a lot done for him in the first several days. But not only was Shana busy, but in the past she'd shown she could be impatient with Tony's shy, unclear way of asking for help. Tony didn't want to face a blow up while he was mending. So he did things for himself that he shouldn't have, fetching things, bending over, putting a strain on himself so that he got re-injured before he'd had time to heal.

None of this is necessary, neither what Amy and Jerry went through, nor what Tony and Shana went through. Yet because we don't know how to get the best out of the people who are there to support us, we add a whole other level of strain and misery to our lives (and theirs), making the second illness far worse. But it doesn't have to be this way.

HAVING A BETTER RELATIONSHIP WITH YOUR CAREGIVERS

We don't want to think that the bonds of love and friendship are so weak that they can be easily frayed by caring for a loved one. Now here's the real truth. The bonds of love and friendship can be *strengthened* by the experience of caring for a loved one. Suppose you knew how to do a great job with the people who are there to support you. Everyone would feel much better. And you really would get better faster.

It's important to understand is that it's up to you to make this work. I know—this seems horribly unfair. There you are, sick or injured, so shouldn't it be up to the people who are taking care of you to make it work? Yes, in an ideal world. But how are you going to change those people. In the real world, it's up to you to make the relationship work if you want to feel cared for. The people in your life love you, and they're concerned for you now that you're sick or injured, but they still have their own lives— and so do you. It's your body that's unwell, and getting better and knowing how to be taken care of yourself is your responsibility.

Maybe this is the best way to put it: Your friends and family do want to help you. If you want the kind of care you feel you deserve, you need to be the kind of patient who will make it likely that you get that kind of care.

172

THE SEVEN PATIENT PECCADILLOES

I once asked caregivers to use one word or phrase that best captured what drove them crazy about the sick or injured they had to deal with. The answers that came up most often were:

- Impatience
- Finicky-ness or perfectionism
- Lack of clarity
- Overloading the caregiver with needs
- Making too big a deal over every little thing
- Not giving enough information
- Anger

If you want to avoid driving your caregiver crazy, avoid doing all seven. Here are some practical tips for how to do that.

HOW TO WIN AT THE BEING-A-PATIENT GAME

Give a daily update/debriefing. You might think this is a strange recommendation to put first. But it's powerfully helpful for everyone. Your spouse/friend/relative needs to know where you're at, but he doesn't need to keep hearing it. You need this person to know where you're at, and you also need him not to get sick of hearing it. The best way to avoid these pitfalls is to limit yourself to one briefing a day at whatever time seems best. State:

- How you're feeling
- Whether or not you're feeling better or worse
- What you might particularly need that day

Be complete, specific, and bring forth everything that's important to you. You'll see—this will make things better for everyone.

Ask clearly and specifically for what you want, and say when you want it. The single most common reason we don't get our needs met when we're under the weather is that we don't have the attention of the person who's caring for us. You might think you do, because it's just the two of you sitting there, but she's got so much on her mind and *you've been talking so much* that your need just doesn't come through loud and clear. So here's a good way to ask for what you need:

> "I need to ask you for something. Is this a good time for you? [Wait for the go ahead.] This is important to me because [and say why this is important to you]. I need you to [state *exactly* what it is you want your caregiver to do]. Do you have any questions? And I need you to do this [state exactly when this needs to be done, whether it's immediately, in the next hour, before the end of the day, whenever]."

I know you're going to say that this is too formal. You're right. Obviously you're not going to go through this to ask someone to hand you a banana. And obviously you can put this into your own words.

But here's the deal. Every time I've seen a disaster where someone who was sick or injured didn't get something she really needed from the person caring for her, and got mad and resentful as a result, it was because she hadn't more or less followed this formula. So don't follow it if you don't want to. But then don't come complaining to me about how the person who's supposed to care for you is never "there" for you!

Assign priorities from 1 to 10. Caregivers complain that it's hard for them to tell how important it is when people ask for something. Big things, little things, it's all a blur. So do yourself a favor. When there's something you want your caregiver to do for you, let him know how important it is to you by giving it a number on a scale from 1 to 10.

For example, you might say, "I'd like you to do something for me. Could you pick up a copy of the new *Oprah* magazine on your way home? On a scale from 1 to 10, this is an 8 for me. It's just come out and I've been looking forward to reading it all day."

Or you might say, "I need you to start cooking healthy food for me—chicken or fish with a lot of vegetables. This is a 10 for me. I'm not going to get better unless I start eating better."

Or you might say, "If you have a chance, please pick up a new murder mystery for me on your way home. It's just a 5 for me—there's still lots to read here, and I'd rather have you home sooner than out looking for a book. But if you have a chance, it would be nice."

By assigning a number you're working out a system with the person who's taking care of you that prevents those relationship-eroding misunderstandings that we've all experienced so many times.

State a need—don't make a complaint. Here's how patients and caregivers work at cross purposes. A patient complains to let his caregiver know what a big deal his need is. His complaints annoy his caregiver and damage her incentive to meet his need. It's tragic, really. People complain, instead of simply saying what they need, because they're afraid that others won't respond to a simple statement of need. But our complaining destroys the very motivation that we're trying to create.

Here's what works. If you're cold, for example, don't waste a minute telling your caregiver how cold you are, how long you've been cold, what terrible things will happen if you stay this cold, what a terrible person she is for letting you get this cold—*none* of that. Just say, "Could you get me a blanket?" or "Could you turn up the thermostat a few degrees?" If you feel you're not getting a response, then instead of *com*plaining, you can *ex*plain why what you're asking for is important to you.

Explain your illness or injury (or have someone do it for you). I'm always surprised how someone can take care of a person with an illness or injury and not appreciate everything that's involved. Usually the first dawn of such appreciation occurs after the patient explodes, saying, "Don't you understand what it's like for me to have to deal with blankety-blank?!" Patients are always amazed at how their caregivers don't "get" what they're going through.

Patients usually make the mistake of assuming their caregiver has full information and bad intentions. The opposite is true. Caregivers almost always have good intentions and poor information. Of course, when patients try to give information, they usually do it at a time when they're upset, and it sounds like complaining. And people don't hear what you say when you complain. They just hear *that* you're complaining.

So for goodness sake, do yourself a favor. Assume that your caregiver really wants to understand what it's like to be going through a difficult pregnancy. Or suffering through migraines. Or having a broken leg. Or dealing with peripheral vascular disease. Just tell your caregiver everything you know about your illness or injury, focusing on the impact it has on you. Pretend you're part of a series where real patients are invited to the nearest medical school to explain to medical students what it's like to actually experience from the inside certain illnesses or injuries. You'll be helping yourself a lot.

Give advance warning of your needs or problems.
It's not always possible to do this, of course. But if you know that you're going to need something, or you know a problem is going to come up, you're more likely to get it, and your caregiver is more likely to be cheerful and unfrazzled, if she has advance warning.

For example, if you're going to the hospital for a test and you want a friend or family member to come with you, make sure you give enough notice so they can schedule it in. But also make clear exactly what you'll need from them when they go with you. Do you need them to stay with you during the test? Do you need them to talk to you or to let you be quiet? Do you want them to ask the doctor questions for you? Do you want them to take notes? Do you want them to talk about your problem, or not?

The one unpardonable sin here is for you to turn the support you need into a guessing game or a game of gotcha. Now, I understand that you don't always know in advance what you're going to need. And I understand that if you say what you need and you don't get it, you might be more disappointed than if you hadn't said it. And I also understand that if someone really, really, *really* loved you they would always know exactly how you feel without your ever having to say anything . . . but of course you know that's not true. And that's my point. There's no escape from you're having to say what it is you need. And since saying what you need in advance vastly increases the likelihood that you'll get it, that's what you should do.

State one need at a time. Caregivers rapidly get confused and overloaded when you state more than one need at a time. And the more important your need, the more important it is that you let it stand alone, highlighted in its pristine isolation. No, don't be ridiculous—if you need some things from the kitchen, you can of course list everything you want.

I know this is hard. We all know what it's like when something goes wrong with our body. Someone says, "How are you feeling?" and a whole bunch of feelings come pouring out: "My head hurts, and my throat hurts, and my rear end hurts from staying in bed so long, and I'm bored. . . ." and on and on. The truth is that the worse you feel, the more different kinds of bad feelings you have and the more needs you have and the more you want someone to make it all go away. If some poor soul should happen to get within earshot of you, out tumbles your long list of needs.

This is fine if all you want is for the other person to listen. But if you actually want to get your needs met, just state one need at a time, and then it's harder for your caregiver to forget or become confused.

Write out schedules and to-do lists. Even caring for someone who has the flu can get surprisingly complicated. No one can remember everything. So get out the old pen and paper and keep two lists.

First write down all the things you need to have done for you. Everything from having your orange juice, coffee, and medicine brought to you in the morning to any shopping you might need to have done.

Then write out a schedule for when to do these things. This is particularly important if your caregiver goes off to work for the day. A written schedule makes it more likely that you'll get your needs met. Knowing when something's going to happen and having it to look forward to provides definite psychological benefits.

Give specific feedback* early *when there's a problem.
It's almost inevitable that you won't get the exact kind of
care you need. Maybe your caregiver is always late with
everything. Or always forgets something. Or the food is
always cold or poorly cooked. Or maybe his manner with
you is too cold or too solicitous or too *something*. The
ground work has been laid for a huge fight.

Now let's see if you can avoid that fight and get your
needs met. The first thing you've got to do is bring up the
problem before you get mad. Too often, we don't say something because we don't want to make a stink or because we
don't think it will do any good, but then when the problem
goes on (and it usually does go on!) we blow up. How
many times are you going to fall into that same trap? Why
not do something different for a change? When you see the
problem, but before you get too mad—that's when you say
something. This will automatically make it easier for your
caregiver to hear what you have to say.

Next, follow this procedure for giving specific feedback:

Say something appreciative: "You've really been trying."
Or, "You've been taking good care of me." Or, "It means a
lot to me, everything you've been doing."

Then say what's been bothering you in the fewest words
possible, without dramatics, without exaggeration. Be specific. Give examples. *And say why this is important to you.*
For example, "The last few days you've seemed so rushed
every time you've had anything to do with me. Like just
before, when I was telling you what I wanted to eat, you
dashed out of here before I finished, the soup wasn't really hot when you brought it to me, and you just sort of

plunked it on the table without helping me sit up. This just makes me feel like I'm a burden to you. And it makes me afraid to ask you for anything."

Then say what you want to be different from now on. Again, the more specific you are, the better. Above all, don't ask the other to be a different kind of person. Don't ask the other to be more "considerate," "caring," "responsible," or anything like that. Instead, talk about the *behaviors* you want to see. Talk about your getting hot meals that are actually hot. Talk about your caregiver sitting with you for a few minutes to chat. Talk about your caregiver writing things down so he won't forget what he's supposed to do.

End by saying something appreciative and encouraging. It would be great if people loved getting feedback, but they don't. So you have to bury the bitterness in sweetness. When I was a kid and my mother wanted me to take aspirin, she'd mash it up in some applesauce. Beginning and ending your feedback with something positive is the applesauce that makes the pill of feedback palatable.

Don't start difficult discussions when either of you is exhausted or in pain. Somewhere along the line, some idiot came up with the idea that you should never go to bed mad. Would someone please find him and give him a dope slap for me? The real truth is that you should never wake up exhausted. And you should never talk about something important when you don't have the time or energy to talk about it. So *never* talk about some problem at night before going to bed. If you go to bed mad, I guarantee that you'll wake up less mad and a lot better rested than if you'd talked the problem to death until three o'clock in the morning. The single best time to talk about problems is after a meal. But you have to do it. You can't wait until things get out of control, because then you'll be too upset to have a good discussion.

***If you need** a lot of care, urge your caregiver to get help*. There's a reason why nurses work shifts. Caregiving chews up caregivers. You might not notice how many demands you're placing on your caregiver if maybe they just do a few things for you in the morning, go off to work, and then do a couple more things in the evening for you. But most of us are already maxed out. Any extra set of demands can soon feel like too much.

Caregiver burnout can be an issue even if you only have the flu—just ask half the spouses in America. But the more serious your illness or injury, the greater the risk you face from the second illness, and yet the more worn out your caregiver may be. Just when you may need the most help, you may be able to get the least from your caregiver. This is why it's so crucial to have friends and relatives to hand off some of the work to, if that's possible.

You have to be particularly wary of how a caregiver who loves you will burn herself out and yet not want to tell you. You may only notice it when you experience a certain level of irritability or sloppiness. And that will make you angry—and that puts your relationship under strain. So you have to make sure your caregiver gets some time off before things get that bad.

Regularly appreciate your caregiver. In the patient/ caregiver relationship, patients often feel inadequately cared for and caregivers often feel underappreciated. Even when patients feel that their caregiver is trying, they feel that on some level he's clueless or callous or hapless, at least to some degree. How do you appreciate someone, then, when you feel at least a little frustrated and deprived?

You praise your caregiver and show gratitude for all the little things he does. You don't even have to actually say the words "thank you." You can just say something like, "Oh, this soup is just what I need now," or "I feel so much more cheerful with those flowers," or "I feel nice and warm now with that extra blanket."

This kind of appreciation will make your caregiver feel he's making a difference. And it will serve as emotional fuel, making it easier for him to keep on taking good care of you.

13

Healing the Patient-Caregiver Relationship

You might think it's weird for me to tell you about all the things you have to do to get the best possible care from the people around you. But this isn't a book for your caregivers. You're the one with the medical problem. And you really don't have control over other people. The only person you have control over is you. I've found that unless someone is in the throes of agony or is pretty much out of it, they still have some control over what they say and how they deal with people.

And I want you to feel that sense of control, even though it may not be easy for you. That's because that sense of control goes very far towards curing your second illness and helping you feel better fast.

The gremlin in the patient/caregiver relationship is humiliation. It's humiliating to be sick or injured. You're reduced to living like a helpless child in some ways, plus you're liable to make funny noises too! Your body is in control, not you, and maybe that's the root of your humiliation. No wonder you're at risk of the second illness.

Now add on to this the fact that someone who cares about you is inevitably dropping the ball in some important ways, as if he . . . *didn't care*. Now you feel doubly humiliated. The only thing that prevents you from getting really sad is your getting really angry.

How do you lift yourself out of this? You've already seen one way—just follow the instructions for how to be a perfect patient. I promise you: the better a patient you are, the better your caregiver will seem to you. But another way is to have a better understanding of what's going on with your caregiver. That will prevent you from feeling humiliated and deprived, and *that* will intercept the stress/discouragement response.

All this was driven home to me when a patient asked me straight out, "Why aren't the people in my life more helpful and supportive?" Beth wasn't complaining. She just wanted to understand. But she'd been going through infertility treatments and she felt no one knew how hard it was for her. In fact she had the sneaking suspicion that her husband, Mike, didn't want to know. Maybe he felt guilty. Maybe "ladies complaints" freaked him out, the way they do for a lot of men. And maybe, like a lot of men and women, too, he didn't seem like he cared simply because he didn't know what to do and say.

But that's just it: he didn't *seem* like he cared. That's why Beth felt he wasn't helpful and supportive, and that's why she was so depressed. "So what if you're going through hell—I just don't care. Ha. Ha. Ha." This is what Mike seemed to be saying to Beth.

But the more I talked to her, the more clear it became that Mike really did care, that he was doing the best he could, and that Beth herself was responsible for some of the ways Mike wasn't doing as good a job as he might have. For example, Beth would do things like waiting to see whether Mike would pick up on her signals, as a way of seeing if he really cared. Beth would say, "I hate to ask for things," but then she'd complain when she didn't get them. Beth would minimize what she was having to deal with physically and then get upset when Mike didn't realize how hard it was for her. Then, of course, the deeper Beth fell into a state of resentment and disappointment, the less Mike wanted to be close to Beth.

What a mess, and yet how typical.

Beth could've saved herself a lot of trouble if she'd taken another look at how she was treating Mike and started giving him the benefit of the doubt. Everyone should do this.

Beth needed to stop thinking of Mike's care-giving as a thermometer showing just how intense his love was, as if the more he loved her the better he would take care of her. The truth is very different. *Because* he loved her, he was there, doing his best to care for her. Beyond that, though, the things he forgot, the things he didn't see, the things he seemed insensitive to were just expressions of how busy, distracted, confused, and limited he was, *just like every other normal, loving human being in the world.*

When Beth changed her attitude and started seeing Mike's care-giving as an expression of love, however imperfect, Beth was able to feel more loved and less humiliated by the level of care poor old Mike was able to give her. The second illness diminished markedly for Beth, just by her realizing this.

Beth also needed to lower her expectations. Now don't misunderstand me. If you're sick or injured, you deserve to be treated well. On the other hand, if you really wanted first-class service, you should've married the head purser on the QE2. And if your spouse just happens to be the QE2's head purser, you know all too well how tired he, too, is when he comes home.

So don't expect perfection. Assume that your caregiver is all Seven Dwarfs wrapped up in one. Yes, Doc and Happy are somewhere in the mixture. But you've also got Dopey, Sleepy, and Grumpy. And don't forget about Bashful and Sneezy. And think about how much they *all* loved Snow White. But even with all seven of them, and all the birds and bunnies helping out, too, Snow White wasn't getting four-star care.

So expect fumbling. Expect forgetfulness. Expect misunderstandings and insensitivity. Expect soup that isn't always as hot as you'd like. And expect dopiness, sleepiness, and grumpiness. But also expect someone who'll show his loving by the way he tries, even if he keeps dropping the ball. And expect from yourself that the more patient you are and the more clearly you ask for what you need, the more likely it is that you'll feel well cared for.

REVEALING THE PERSON INSIDE THE PATIENT

You know how people sometimes say beware of what you wish for, you just might get it? That happens sometimes with caregivers. They put you in the patient box, lock in on what's wrong with you, and throw away the key. In other words, they treat you like a patient, not a person. You're getting really good care, and yet you feel lonely and somehow shunted off to the side.

"No one treats me the same way any more," Harvey said after his heart attack. He was a very young man to have had a heart attack, but while that made for a better prognosis, it threw his family for a loop. They couldn't stop thinking of him as an invalid—damaged goods. All they could see was a guy who might drop dead any moment if subjected to the slightest stress or exertion.

"Don't bother your father," his wife Emma kept saying to the boys. In the evening they'd stay away from him. They'd walk past the room he was in, wave through the doorway, and move on. Emma fed Harvey like a king, a king on a distinctly heart-friendly diet. But she stopped talking to him. She was afraid that at any moment she might stumble into saying something that would upset him.

Heart patients often deal with depression. But it was

being treated like this that made Harvey depressed. When I told Emma that she needed to start treating Harvey more like a normal guy, she said something like what everyone in her situation says: "The minute I start treating him regular, he's going to complain I'm giving him a heart attack." But this is really just a version of saying, hey, you can't win, so why try.

Here's what I said to Emma and Harvey, and here's what you and your caregiver should know if you're in this situation.

Everyone *can* win at this business of treating someone like a person and a patient at the same time, and you should try. You just won't be perfect, that's all. No one can be perfect.

To illustrate, just think about people who are *dying*. Now everyone's different, but most of the people in this situation want the people around them to be friendly, cheerful, relaxed. They want them to chat about everyday things, gossip, politics, fashions, sports, and it's okay if they talk about who might end up playing in a World Series they'll never get to see.

At the same time they don't want the fact that they're dying to be ignored. That's real, too. They need to be asked if there's anything they especially want to talk about. They need to be encouraged to make special requests. They need to be given full space to talk about their feelings.

If you can treat someone who's dying like a person and a patient at the same time, then you can do it with someone who's grumpy because she has an ulcer or a kidney condition.

HOW NOT TO GET POLARIZED

The most common dynamic that arises between patient and caregiver is what I call maximizing/minimizing. It's just another way people get polarized. The way it works is . . . well, why don't I show you with this little playlet:

> *Patient* (not feeling that the caregiver has been sufficiently attentive): Don't you understand how hard it is for me to do anything for myself now?
>
> *Caregiver*: I don't understand why you make such a big deal of this. The doctor told you to stay off your feet—she didn't tell you that you couldn't get out of bed at all.
>
> *Patient*: Don't you get it—I'm in constant pain. And I'm never going to get better if I have to keep running around doing things that you're supposed to be doing for me.
>
> *Caregiver*: There's not that much wrong with you. There's no way you can be in so much pain. I mean, come on, it's not that big a deal.
>
> *Patient*: God, you're such a bastard.
>
> *Caregiver*: No, I'm just trying to be realistic. You're the one who's being a big baby.

And that's how these things always end. One person ends up labeled a bastard, the other a baby.

Here are the ingredients in this sad dynamic. One person feels a little uncared for, the other feels a little put upon. The patient decides he's going to "teach" the caregiver to be more considerate and sensitive. He does this by holding up a mirror showing the caregiver how inconsiderate and insensitive she's been. The caregiver decides that, no, it's the patient who needs to learn to be stronger and more self reliant. She does this by trying to show the patient how weak and demanding he's been.

Both people feel the monstrous unfairness of these accusations.

> "I'm your caregiver, and you're calling me *inconsiderate and insensitive?! After all I've done for you?! What a baby you are!"*
>
> "I'm sick, and you're calling me *weak and demanding?! With all the suffering and problems I have to deal with?! What a bastard you are!"*

I think most of us who've either been under the weather for any period of time or who've had to care for someone like this will recognize this dynamic.

But this dynamic is really a paper tiger. Here's how to bat it out of the way so it doesn't afflict your relationship. If you, the patient, feel your caregiver is being insensitive and inconsiderate, don't yell at him for being insensitive and inconsiderate. You're just going to end up being called a baby two or three steps down the line. Instead, carefully follow the instructions above for how to be the perfect patient. That way you'll elicit all the sensitivity and consideration you could possibly want.

A very simple, straightforward way of getting what you need is to zero in on what your caregiver is specifically doing that makes you think he's insensitive and inconsiderate. Maybe it's how he leaves the house early in the morning without asking you if there's anything you need before he goes. Maybe it's how he doesn't return your call during the day. Maybe it's how he comes home late, leaving you sitting there hungry. Whatever it is, use the magic phrase:

> It's really important to me—it's a 10—that you ask me if there's anything I need before you dash off in the morning [or whatever it is that's really bugging you]. *What do you need to be able to do that for me?*

Now here's the magic *in* this phrase. Instead of heading down the trail of calling him a bastard and getting called a baby, *you're asking him what he needs*. This flips the dynamic around completely. You're offering to give something at precisely the moment when you don't feel given to. Is that crazy? No, it *works* like crazy. Try it. You'll see.

TUNING IN TO YOUR CAREGIVER

Here's a simple and powerful tool for dealing with the person who's taking care of you when you're sick or injured.

193

Do an even better job than you've been doing of listening to *him*. If you really listen, and show you've really heard, this will open the door to his hearing you.

Listening means getting a better sense of where the other person is coming from. Here are some questions you can ask:

- How do you understand what's going on with my body?
- What do you expect is going to happen over time with me?
- What kind of help do you need, and how can I help you help me?
- What are you afraid of about my illness?
- What are the biggest problems you think I'm having to deal with?
- What do you think my needs are?
- How do you think I want to be treated?

Years of experience have taught me that your asking these questions and listening until you get full answers to each question is the best way to guarantee that eventually *you* will be heard. Open mouths generate closed ears. But open ears generate more open ears. Your anger will diminish. The people in your life will do a better and better job of meeting your needs. And because you're not so angry, they'll be more willing to talk to you and help you, which will accelerate even further their doing a better job.

SOLDIERS AND BABIES

When do you baby yourself? When do you soldier on? This issue comes up surprisingly quickly and with great emotional weight whenever something goes wrong with our bodies, and it can play havoc with your relationship with your caregiver. The temptation to take time out from work and have people run around fetching things for you is enormous. On the other hand, it's easy to feel very guilty about doing anything other than carrying on just the way you did before. Sometimes you find that someone's mad at you no matter what you do.

There's no question about it: When our bodies get into trouble, we have to be *both* soldiers *and* babies. What's good about soldiers is that they're stoical, and they refuse to let themselves be defined by what's wrong with them. Their assumption is, if you can, you do. But babies have something to teach us also. Our needs and limitations are very real, and we're often much more vulnerable than we think. Bad things happen when care isn't taken of the sick or injured, no less than babies.

Three rules of thumb should guide you here:

- Action is better than inaction.
- If you need to be taken care of, then you need to be taken care of.
- Don't do anything that will cause more problems.

We now know that, in general, the more active sick and injured people are, the better. That's why they get post-op patients and post-delivery moms moving rapidly—it's not just for the hospital's convenience. And it feels better psychologically to move, too. I know it's nice to be waited on hand and foot, but people really do feel better when they get up to make their own sandwich or to get themselves cleaned up than when someone does it for them.

You have to think about the people around you, too. They can be as loving and giving as you could want. But they're not bottomless wells. And they have an instinct for when you're trying to get them to do something you could perfectly well do yourself. They might put up with your crossing the line once or twice, but if you keep asking people to do for you things you can do for yourself, you'll wear out the patience of people you may really need to be there for you at some other time.

But don't run around just for public relations sake. There are times when we need to be taken care of. We're literally too weak to make food for ourselves. Too much in pain to walk around. Too fragile to take a shower. If you soldier on in a situation like this, you're just making things worse.

In general you need to baby yourself if being active will make problems. For example, don't go to work if you're contagious. How does your being on the job for one day make up for your knocking five of your fellow employees off the job? Don't go to work if you're bleary and you need to make tough decisions. Don't go to work if you need to function at a high level and whatever is wrong with you will prevent you from doing so.

And don't go to work if running around will set you back in your recovery. This is particularly important with injuries. There's always a period when you feel better but you're still fragile. This is when people consistently re-injure themselves by pushing too hard too fast.

14
Making Sure You Get the Optimal Treatment

You're at risk for the second illness if you passively submit to the "treatment lottery," taking whatever kind of care happens to be offered to you. But you will feel better and get better faster if you understand that you can be in charge of your getting the best possible care.

Sometimes that can be frustrating.

"Did you get a load of those clowns walking around on our roof?" I asked my wife. We'd suddenly developed a bad leak in the roof of our hundred-year-old house, and the people I'd hired to fix it didn't make me feel confident that they could do a good job. But they were the only ones I could get. In our area, it's tough to find a good roofer. And so there I was, feeling like a sucker and a victim, with some clowns walking around on my roof.

We've all been in situations like that. Something goes wrong and all you know is that some clowns are going to cost you a lot of money and that you may be left with the same problems you started with. It makes you feel angry, apprehensive, and discouraged.

That's how it goes for many of us when we get sick or injured. It's great if you have a primary care physician you have a good relationship with and you've come to trust the specialists you're seeing. But at some point, if your illness or injury is at all serious or complicated, it's very easy to start wondering if the doctor you want to trust really knows what he's doing and has your best interests at heart (as opposed to his keeping to his schedule, or holding costs down, or not getting in trouble with the HMO for referring too many people on). Then there you are again wondering who those clowns are walking around on your roof.

When you're sick or injured, you need help. Nothing will make you feel more helpless at that point than your not getting the kind of treatment you need and want. But then nothing will help you feel better fast than feeling you're in charge of the kind of treatment you get.

WHEN YOU NEED TREATMENT

A well connected woman who was dealing with a serious illness stunned me the other day when she said bluntly,

"Everyone I know hates their doctors." Whoa! Understand that the people she knows are well placed men and women here in Boston who have access to some of the best medical care in the world.

But you can see where she's coming from. When you take overworked, overspecialized doctors, throw them together with sophisticated patients with sky-high expectations, and stir a Byzantine health-care system into the mix, you have a recipe for a crisis in doctor/patient relations.

There are many exceptions to this generality, of course, but we've come to realize that people are not getting the *sense of care* from their doctors that they need and have a right to expect. And all this is because the emotional aspects of your situation are neglected. You are being treated like a body according to the doctor's priorities, not like a person according to your priorities. Here's an example of this.

Jane, 45, went through an experience most of us can identify with. She innocently mentioned to her internist that she'd had "one drop of blood" on her panties between periods. She'd always been very regular, and there was no chance she could be pregnant. The internist, playing defensive medicine the way so many doctors do these days, sent Jane to an ob/gyn to have this checked out.

The ob/gyn treated her impersonally. She ordered a series of tests, starting with a pelvic ultrasound. The ultrasound results were just ambiguous enough for the ob/gyn to want to perform a uterine biopsy. It hurt Jane a lot. The results of the biopsies on these tissue samples were also ambiguous.

So now an in-patient procedure was scheduled. The ob/gyn figured that since they weren't sure exactly what they were dealing with, they should scrape away all of the lining of the uterus. That way if there was anything cancerous starting to grow there, it would be removed. In the end they found nothing to worry about. Everything was fine.

All these procedures had been unnecessary. Throughout, Jane felt like a shuttlecock in a medical badminton game. "By the time it was all over, I wondered if anything that had happened had anything to do with me. Not once at any point was I consulted about how I felt, what my priorities were, and what I needed as I was going though this rigmarole."

No wonder so many of us think, "Hey wait a minute— I'm the patient here, it's my body, my discomfort, my fear, and yet I'm made to feel like some lowly deckhand on the ship of medicine."

There comes a time when we all feel it's really hard to be a patient. You don't feel understood. You don't feel listened to. You don't feel you're being treated as an individual. You don't feel you're being taken seriously. You're not even sure the doctor "gets" what's really wrong with you. This is when everything about your treatment starts feeling frustrating, confusing, overwhelming.

It's stressful to feel in the dark and not have a sense of control. It's humiliating not to be treated with respect. Both of these occur when you're not given full information and don't have a say in your health-care decisions. Stress plus humiliation adds up to a real case of the second illness.

TAKING BACK THE POWER

Here's how to feel more effective and *be* more effective with your treatment. This will go far towards curing the second illness, but it will do even more than that. The more effective you are as a patient, the more likely you are to recover faster and more completely from whatever has gone wrong with your body.

Throw out your old ways of dealing with what's going on when you get sick or injured. The truth is that when something goes wrong with our body, we feel helpless, and we act that way. We instinctively look for someone we can trust who can make everything better for us. In other words, we act like children. Sometimes this approach works, and when it does, it's great. But if it were that easy, no one would ever suffer from the second illness.

You know what they say: if something doesn't work and you keep on doing it anyway, that's just crazy! So let's admit that it's crazy when something goes wrong with your body to start out feeling helpless and turn over all the responsibility to your doctor and others. That's just acting as if you really were helpless. And in the long run, that just makes you feel worse.

The best way to think about getting sick or injured is to think of it as a project you've been hired to manage and your doctors are your employees.

So let's get to work.

RULES FOR MANAGING YOUR DOCTOR

Here's what you need to understand if you want to do a great job managing the doctors you've "hired" to help you get well.

Your doctors will appreciate you and will do a better job if you're informed, active, and involved in your health care. I understand, of course, that doctors don't like patients who are bossy and try to micro-manage them. And I understand that doctors themselves can be pretty bossy or aloof towards you. But there are plenty of studies that show that the patients who get the best care are the ones who take the most responsibility for their health care. Maybe this is a case of "God helps those who help themselves."

One study tried to determine if there were racial differences in the way people were treated in a large cardiology clinic, perhaps as a result of unconscious racism on the part of doctors. In this very careful study, they did find differences in the way people were treated, but not based on race.

The difference was based on the degree to which patients took on the role of full, active partners in their recovery. Active patients who worked to form a full partnership with their doctor draw the best care. These patients complied best with their doctor's instructions, but they also asked the most questions and worked hardest to draw the doctor most closely into the reality of their lives by giving relevant information about whatever special needs they had and whatever unusual situations they might be facing.

If you're satisfied with the progress you're making and the treatment you're getting, *this is all you have to do.* It's actually not all that hard. Like a good manager, you've delegated responsibility to your doctor, and as long as he delivers, you stay active and involved but you let him do his job.

But what if you're not satisfied with your progress or the treatment you're getting? Well, you have a choice. You can suffer and get frustrated. But then the second illness and your primary condition are both at risk of deteriorating. Or you can kick it up a notch. I realize we'd all prefer to let the doctor be in the driver's seat. It makes us uncomfortable to think about grabbing the wheel. But what else can you do if you're not happy with the way things are going? You can stay unhappy *or you can act.*

And then the following principles come into play.

You're the person ultimately responsible for your getting better, not your doctor, not your spouse, not anyone else. Don't confuse expertise with responsibility. Of course your doctor has more medical knowledge than you do. That's why you've hired him or her! But that's the point: your doctor works for you, not the other way around. You're the person who suffers if your recovery is delayed. So you're in charge. Everyone else is there to help you.

You can only manage your team well if you're well informed about your condition. You're not going to go to medical school when something goes wrong with your body. But between using the library, looking things up on the Internet, and calling experts on the telephone, you can learn a stunning amount of information that will assist you in questioning the usefulness and safety of the procedures and medications your doctor is prescribing.

You have to assert yourself. When you bring up your concerns about your treatment or mention alternative treatments, you're not "challenging your doctor's authority." You're just asking questions. And then you ought to expect a response that's intelligent, thorough, and takes your concerns seriously. For example, you might say, "I was reading about that procedure you recommended. A couple of articles I saw said there were real risks with it and that in fact most people ended up doing just as well with medication and physical therapy. What's your thinking about why I personally would be best off with that procedure?" And then don't get sidelined or put off until you feel you've gotten an answer that addresses and quiets your concerns.

Being assertive doesn't mean being a pushy jerk. It's just that you know your body and how you feel. You understand your life and what you want from your life. You've learned a great deal about your condition. Knowing all this, you're in a position to say exactly what it is you want and to hang in there asking for what you want until you either get it or have a damned good reason for why you can't get it.

Making Sure You Get the Optimal Treatment

It's all about the relationship. As long as your doctor is competent and experienced, the most important thing is finding a doctor you like and respect and who likes and respects you. In my experience, most successful cures grow out of this relationship of mutual liking and respect.

If you can't have this kind of relationship with your doctor, because one of you doesn't like or respect the other, then find a doctor you can have this kind of relationship with. It's not a luxury. It's a necessity. When liking and respect are absent from both sides of the patient/doctor relationship, the result is substandard care.

Now most doctors have professional manners that are either blandly pleasant or reserved and businesslike. It would be pretty unusual to find a doctor who acts like it makes his day when he sees you. But you *certainly* should never have a doctor who you feel actually dislikes you.

And some of this is your responsibility. Of course, no one expects someone who's feeling lousy to be Ms. or Mr. Congeniality. You don't have to tap dance. You don't have to subordinate your needs in the interests of likeability. But you help yourself a lot if you act as friendly as possible and treat your doctor like a person as opposed to a machine or an underling. With my own patients, some walk in the room and ask me how I'm doing and some don't. I automatically feel better about patients who make a polite gesture of being interested in me as a person. We're human beings, too. We can't help but respond to a minimal attempt at friendliness.

SIZING UP YOUR DOCTOR

It's comforting to feel you have a good relationship with a good doctor, and to feel that what you do to be informed and involved with your treatment is welcomed. But the more this is *not* true, the more you're liable to feel stressed and discouraged. And then your doctor is *giving you* a case of the second illness.

This can be scary and confusing. For one thing, we're usually not sure whether our issues with the doctor are as bad as we're afraid they are. Dr. Jones consistently dismisses your concerns . . . but maybe your concerns are overanxious and ill informed. Dr. Smith is an aloof, cold fish, and you don't feel you can really open up to her . . . but you think maybe it's okay, because that's how really, really smart doctors behave. Dr. Miller never has time for you . . . but maybe you're too demanding, and maybe his being so busy is a sign that he's a great doctor.

For many people, the more vulnerable you feel because of your illness or injury, the scarier it is to think about firing your doctor. And the longer this person has been your doctor, the more you may feel that they know you so well that you shouldn't bother starting up with someone new. So what do you do? It can be emotionally exhausting to search for a new doctor, but it's also emotionally exhausting—and maybe dangerous—to stay with a doctor who isn't right for you.

Here's how to sort all this out.

GRADING YOUR DOCTOR

You deserve to be free from anxiety about the care you're getting. If you try to find the absolute best doctor, you'll just be setting yourself up for endless anxiety. What I recommend instead is what I call "the good enough doctor for you." You should feel that your doctor is good enough for you as long as he or she gets a passing grade on all of the following criteria.

Big ears. The best doctors are the ones who really listen. They may walk into the room reading your chart, but they ask you what's going on, and they really listen to your answer. And then when they examine you, you feel that they really have heard you. When they ask you a question, they follow up your answers with more questions. You can sense them thinking about what you say like a detective following up on clues.

Respect. The best doctors treat you like a sane, intelligent person. Not like a hysteric, an idiot, or a child. You should *not* feel that your doctor thinks that you're exaggerating your symptoms. You should *not* feel that your doctor is explaining away your complaints, for example by saying that they are due to the fact that you're female (if you are female of course!) or that you're just someone who's anxious or stressed out.

Big heart. You need to feel that your doctor has a big heart. That means that her diagnosis and treatment are based as much on her understanding of who you are and what you need as a person as it is on what the textbook says.

Open mind. You don't want a doctor who's open to every crackpot idea or who jumps on every faddish bandwagon. But new treatments, new understandings of what's wrong with you, and alternative approaches should not be discounted or dismissed out of hand. You want a doctor who will have an adult conversation with you about these options, even if ultimately he deems that they're not appropriate in your case. And you want someone who's willing to try new things, provided they don't interfere with best medical practice or cause any actual harm.

Someone who remembers you. If you go to see your doctor and you have a sense that your doctor just doesn't remember you, that's a problem. I know doctors have lots of patients these days. But here's how it works. Before you walk in for a visit after being seen the first time, there's a chart. The doctor should have read the chart, and, unless that doctor doesn't care about people, reading the chart should refresh him about who you are.

Experience. Experience is the single biggest predictor of medical success. Hospitals that do a lot of open-heart surgery have the highest survival rate. Psychotherapists who've worked the longest with certain populations or problems have the highest cure rates. The key is to get specific. You want to make sure that when you select a primary-care physician your doctor has specific experience with your greatest area of concern. You do *not* need a doctor who's in some magazine's list of the best doctors in your city. (A lot of people I know haven't had great experiences with over-hyped doctors.) You do *not* need a doctor who's a medical-school professor. You do *not* need a doctor who has a fancy office at a prestigious address. Your doctor will be plenty good enough if she has seen and is continuing to see a lot of people like you.

Responsiveness. You're entitled to call your doctor if you have a question that's important to you, and you're entitled to get a call back within a day or two, depending on how important your question is. If your doctor is too busy to get back to you to answer an important question, then that doctor's too busy to have you on his patient list.

General openness. Some doctors act like they're working for the CIA. They just don't want to give you information. It's like pulling teeth to get them to tell you your lab results. Or your last blood pressure reading. Or the side effects of the drug they're prescribing. Or what they think might be wrong with you. You don't want a doctor like this. Instead, you want to hear from your doctor words such as these: "Right now, I'm thinking that you probably just have a bad case of X, because only your A is elevated and your B and C are normal. But your D is rather high, and that makes me afraid that you just might have a case of Y, which can be kind of serious. That's why I want to send you to the lab for a couple of other tests so we can rule out Y. In the meantime, I'm going to immediately start treating you for X. Do you have any questions?" The point is that this doctor has shared his knowledge and thought processes with you, and that makes you a better patient and works to relieve your anxiety.

Empathy. You want a doctor who empathizes with your concerns. If some procedure is going to hurt, your doctor lets you know what to expect, because she knows that she wouldn't want to have some painful experience sprung on her. If she has bad news to tell you, she tells you in a way that shows that she understands what it's like to hear news like this. You can't probe your doctor's heart, but you can know whether or not you're being treated the way you're sure your doctor would want to be treated himself.

Custom tailoring. You should never feel like you're *just* a body and numbers on a chart. You don't want to see someone who practices off-the-rack medicine. Even if you have a plain old garden-variety case of strep throat or a sprained ankle, you want to feel that your doctor is sensitive to your medical issues (allergies to certain antibiotics, susceptibility to certain side effects). You also want to feel that he's sensitive to your life style issues—is it a big deal for you to miss work or not, is money a problem for you, are there people in your life who can take care of you? And if your doctor doesn't bring up these issues himself, then he's responsive and respectful when you bring them up.

Making Sure You Get the Optimal Treatment

You're on the same wavelength. Medicine is not an exact science. Attitudes, beliefs, and preferences play a big role, and there's often no right or wrong with them. For example, you might be most comfortable with a doctor who takes what's called a conservative approach, which in medicine means watching and waiting a little while before intervening. Or you might be very much in favor of natural and dietary healing approaches. A doctor who is good enough for you will be one whose attitudes, beliefs, and preferences are roughly in sync with yours.

What do you do if your doctor doesn't live up to these criteria?

Let's not forget that we're talking about a doctor who's good enough for you. No doctor's perfect. No doctor will get an A for each of these criteria. As long as your doctor gets a C or better for these criteria, then you have nothing to worry about. It's even better if he gets a really good grade for whatever criteria are particularly important to you.

If your otherwise-satisfactory doctor fails to live up to any of these standards, give him a chance to redeem himself. I'm not talking about a big confrontation. Instead, I'm talking about saying something like this: "You seemed really busy and distracted the last time I saw you. Honestly, I didn't feel you were listening to me. It's really important to me that I feel listened to." I know it's hard for a lot of us to say something like this. But remember that curing yourself of the second illness depends upon all the ways you empower yourself. Even if it's a little scary to assert your needs like this, I'm sure you'll feel better after you do it.

Then see how your doctor responds. If he makes you feel like you're a ridiculous person for bringing up this issue, that's serious. But if your doctor acknowledges that you have a right to be heard on this topic and indicates that he'll try to do a better job in the future, then that's a good sign.

15

Getting the Most from Your Doctor

Your doctor is the only thing that can come close to making you feel as helpless as your body does. That's why your doctor can be exacerbating your second illness while at the same time he's helping heal your physical illness or injury. He doesn't want to create emotional fall-out. It just happens while his attention is focused on what's wrong with you physically.

Here's how you can eliminate the emotional fallout that grows out of the doctor–patient relationship.

Begin by understanding why it makes sense for you to relax.

You're the recipient of the best medical care in the history of the world. Of course you realize that cures today are often neither as complete nor as straightforward as you'd like. Medicine is still far from perfect. But that doesn't contradict the fact that miracles happen in doctors' offices every day. When your doctor begins an examination by asking what's wrong with you, inside she's feeling confident that she'll be able to diagnose, treat, and cure you. This is why you should relax.

PEOPLE ARE FROM EARTH, DOCTORS ARE FROM PLUTO

Once you have a good doctor, what do you do with him? Some people think you just show up for an appointment, complain about how you feel, and submit to having weird things done to your body. You hope you'll be able to walk out with a prescription.

But there's more to it than that. The patient–doctor relationship is a difficult one. As people, doctors are just like the rest of us. But as doctors, the two of you don't speak the same language, even if you think you do. You have very different needs. And you don't even necessarily understand things the same way.

Here are the important issues that might come up in your relationship and the best ways to deal with them to prevent the stress-discouragement response from kicking in.

GETTING RESULTS THROUGH COMMUNICATION

I have a radical approach to patient–doctor communication. The key is that *your appointment isn't over until you've gotten all your important questions answered clearly and completely. If you've been told more than you can possibly remember, you've gotten a chance to write down everything you need to know.*

Think about what this means. It's not your body, it's not your doctor's schedule, it's not the procedures he follows that determine what your appointment's about. What your appointment really is about is your questions. If you walk out without good answers, you're either going to be filled with fear (there's the second illness again!) or you won't know how to comply with your doctor's instructions.

Here are the questions you should have answers to before you leave:

"What exactly is wrong with me?" You're not just looking for the name of your illness or injury, although that helps, because it provides the basis for your doing research. But you're also looking for some understanding of how your condition works. Where does it come from? What can you expect over time—total cure, muddling along, death, symptom relief, what? And what should you expect you'll have to deal with before you start improving?

"Why am I getting the treatment I'm getting?"
There's rarely just one treatment for the things that go wrong with us. But the treatment your doctor chooses for you is usually based on some priority your doctor has in mind. *But that may not be your priority.* And you need to bring your priorities and your doctor's out into the open. Otherwise, your needs won't be addressed.

Alice went in for a mammogram and was told by the radiologist that there were spots he "didn't like." She was sent to a noted breast surgeon who urged her to undergo a lumpectomy. But Alice knew that her appointment would not be over until she'd asked all her questions. When she asked why she had to have a lumpectomy, the surgeon replied, "So you won't worry."

That was a terrible answer, as far as Alice was concerned. She didn't want to cut off her body parts so she wouldn't have to worry about them! She was worried about people cutting off her body parts! Most important, the doctor hadn't really answered her question. He'd given a psychological answer to a medical question. Alice's top priority was assessing the medical risks correctly.

Those "spots" the radiologist didn't like constituted a potentially serious medical condition. Since there was a threat that Alice could have a significant problem, she was at risk of developing a real second illness even if the physical illness ultimately turned out to be a false alarm. And so no matter what, Alice needed to empower herself to prevent the second illness.

Alice did the right thing. When she saw that she wasn't getting a good answer to her questions, she went to another doctor. He spent much more time explaining the options and risks. It turned out that the odds were against these spots being cancerous, and even if they were cancerous, the odds were against this being a fast-growing cancer. There was every reason to wait and watch. That's what Alice did. And the spots turned out to be benign. Just as important, during this ordeal Alice minimized her stress and discouragement by taking charge the way she did.

Another woman might've had very different priorities. Another woman might be so afraid of the possibility of dying that the risk of removing a possibly healthy body part was worth it if she'd be able to worry less about dying.

No one can tell you what your priorities should be. But you always have to make your priorities clear and understand your doctor's priorities. Your doctor may prescribe a certain drug because he's concerned about the side effect of an alternative drug. But you may not care about those side effects. Your doctor may prescribe a test "just to make sure." But that may be the kind of test you have to pay for out of pocket, and it may be a lot of money for you to spend "just to make sure." If you level with yourself and make sure that your doctor is leveling with you, you'll feel better.

"What is your approach to my problem?" There's a good reason why you can't just buy a few medical textbooks and set yourself up as a doctor—besides the fact that you'd end up going to jail. Medicine isn't like cooking. Both diseases (and injuries) and their treatments have implications that aren't obvious unless you have a lot of experience.

For a certain disease, drugs and surgery might seem like equally effective alternatives, so you'd think your doctor would opt for drugs because they're cheaper. But maybe the long-term results with drug therapy aren't so great. Maybe people who start out taking that drug almost always end up in surgery anyway, but then the problem is worse. So your doctor might prescribe surgery because he knows how things will probably play out.

For another disease, surgery might seem like the most effective alternative. But your doctor may know that for most people with symptoms like yours, once the surgeon gets in there, he usually can't find much of a problem. So there's actually a lot of unnecessary surgery. This is why your doctor may want to wait to make sure that surgery is truly necessary.

These are judgment calls, *and that's what doctors do*. But unless you understand why your doctor is making a particular judgment call, you'll feel like a junior partner in your own health care, and that puts you at risk of the second illness.

IT'S ALL ABOUT YOUR GETTING BETTER

Even if you have the best relationship with the best doctor, it can happen that you won't seem to be getting better fast enough, or better at all in some cases. This can be very scary and have plenty of negative psychological effects. So what do you do when your treatment doesn't seem to work?

Before you hit the panic button or blame your doctor, you need to understand one of medicine's dirty little secrets. *All treatment is experimental.* Even the most tried-and-true drugs, for example, are only proven effective across a sample of individuals. But you're unique. The drug that may be so effective and reliable in general is of unknown effectiveness and reliability when it comes to you and the way your body works. The same thing is true for all operations and all interventions of any kind.

This means that "not making progress" isn't necessarily a statement about you or your illness or injury, or your treatment or your doctor. It's a statement about where you are in an essentially experimental process to determine the best treatment for you. You feel helpless because something you thought would work hasn't. But that may be par for the course.

Tom, 32, only smoked occasionally. Still, when he noticed he was waking up coughing and bringing up phlegm, he chalked it up to smoker's cough. When this went on for a while, he told his doctor about it, and his doctor made the obvious prescription: stop smoking! Tom figured this would do the trick. He quit, but he didn't get better the way he thought he would. Most days, Tom woke up in a coughing fit.

This went on for a long time before Tom went back to his doctor. His doctor saw that Tom was actually suffering from chronic bronchitis. He prescribed an antibiotic, but the antibiotic didn't help Tom as much as his doctor had hoped, perhaps because in Tom's case the underlying infection was viral, not bacterial, and viral infections don't respond to antibiotics.

Tom started falling into a state of anxiety and depression. He was afraid that an incompetent doctor had saddled him with a fatal disease that could've been cured if it had been handled properly from the beginning.

Eventually, Tom was in really bad shape, more emotionally than physically, although his coughing and bringing up phlegm were still bothering him a lot. His sister became so concerned that she called Tom's doctor, and he had Tom come in for a visit.

He laid his cards on the table. "Tom, I'm sorry I didn't stay more on top of this, but when I didn't hear from you, I assumed that you were getting better. The truth is that chronic bronchitis is a bitch to diagnose and treat. I'm not saying we can't beat it. We can. You're still in an early stage. But there's not one clear path to treatment that physicians agree on. This is just one of those situations where we all feel our way. But there are plenty of things we can do. We just have to hang in there and do them. I need you to keep on my tail if something I prescribe doesn't seem to be working."

It's interesting how much better Tom felt after this conversation. People don't need there to be a magic bullet to feel hopeful and effective when it comes to their medical problem. They just need to feel that their doctor is keeping them in the loop, that he cares about them, and that there are always new possibilities.

You can feel hopeful and effective by understanding that there are probably many options still available to you. Like Tom, you've just begun! But you have to be an active participant to make sure you move through this experimental treatment process expeditiously until you're cured. This means talking to your doctor promptly when you discover that the medicine isn't working or that you're having trouble with the side effects.

Modern medicine can work miracles. But it's only in some cases that the doctor hits the bulls eye with the first shot. If you understand how this works, you'll be less susceptible to the second illness. By embracing the process and taking an active role, you become an empowered part of your treatment team. Your sense of helplessness is destroyed.

DEALING WITH EMBARRASSMENT

Most of us have a level of embarrassment about what we bring to our doctors. We tell ourselves that we shouldn't be embarrassed, that the doctor's seen it all a million times. But we're embarrassed anyway. This wouldn't matter if it were just a feeling, but as a result of feeling embarrassed we hide things. This solves our embarrassment problem. But it doesn't solve our *getting better* problem.

If you want to feel better fast, give your doctor full, current information. I understand that there are things about our bodies and our lives that not only embarrass us—we're deeply ashamed of them. Well I have to tell you: nothing could be more normal than having things about yourself that you're deeply ashamed of. Everyone has these things. Things you've done. Things that have happened to you. Things that are going on with your body. But if you suspect that they might be relevant to your medical picture, you have to tell your doctor.

Don't expect the doctor to come to your rescue. She can't guess at what embarrassing material you're keeping silent about. And she's just human—even if she has a suspicion, she may be reluctant to embarrass you. Meanwhile, time gets wasted, and you feel worse.

Let me help you overcome your feelings of embarrassment. I'm not going to tell you that your doctor has seen it all a million times, although if you are seeing an experienced doctor, she almost certainly has seen it more times than you could possibly imagine.

I will tell you how your doctor thinks about the stuff that embarrasses you. *He's grateful to you for sharing it.* You might be surprised that gratitude is his response, but just think about it for a moment. Maybe you've just offered him a key to a puzzle he's been trying to solve. Maybe you've given him an opportunity to feel good about himself for dealing with a problem he actually finds rather easy. Maybe you've given him a chance to reassure you, and doctors always like to give good news.

To patients, doctors look like they're probing, as if they're playing a game of gotcha. To the doctor, though, it feels like problem solving, and that's why he's likely to be grateful for your embarrassing disclosure. To solve a puzzle *and* help a person—that's why people become doctors.

One thing many people are embarrassed about is their fear of pain and discomfort. They don't want to be seen as wusses or wear out their doctor's patience. But you should always ask your doctor about what level of discomfort is common with your treatment, and what kind of discomfort. He won't think you're a baby. And if you do this, you'll be reminding your doctor that discomfort is an issue for you, and so she needs to take that into account. Plus, the first step in pain management, both physiologically and psychologically, is getting ahead of the pain curve with pain management. You can only do that if you know what to expect.

And if it looks like there's going to be more discomfort than you'd like, tell your doctor that you want to take an aggressive approach to pain management and ask what your options are.

BUILDING TRUST

Any time there's an imbalance of power and knowledge between you and someone else, there's a likelihood of mistrust, even if no one actually violates anyone's trust. It's just that your perceptions are so different that mistrust can easily occur. Then if you add in uncertainty, it's almost guaranteed that somewhere along the line something will happen that will cause a loss of trust.

Unequal power. Unequal knowledge. Uncertainty. These are three unavoidable ingredients in every patient–doctor relationship. It's helpful to know that it's perfectly natural for things to happen that will make you mistrust your doctor.

Maybe your doctor doesn't tell you about a treatment option. When you find out about it, you feel betrayed. Maybe your doctor keeps telling you that you're going to get better "soon," but soon never seems to arrive. I know a doctor who injured himself badly when he was accidentally knocked down. His doctor told him that he'd be fine in a couple of weeks. Then his doctor said a couple of months. Then many months. If a doctor can feel strung along, we can all feel strung along.

And maybe your doctor flat out screws up, perhaps by misdiagnosing your illness or injury. I'm not talking about malpractice here. He's followed the right procedures, made the kind of judgment call doctors are forced to make, and he simply got it wrong. How do you trust a doctor who isn't perfect? How do you know he won't screw up again?

Mistrust is a kind of relationship cancer. This is a time for being tough minded. The question you have to ask yourself is: "Does this mistake reveal something bad about my doctor, or does it simply reveal that he's not perfect?"

If you answer this question honestly and sincerely, using appropriate standards, you'll see where to go. For example, if with the symptoms you brought your doctor there were two different diagnoses a doctor could reasonably make, and your doctor selected the wrong one, it's hard to see how this reveals a flaw in your doctor. But I had a dentist once who was recommending treatments far more expensive than what I really needed. This wasn't a judgment call. This was an attempt to pick my pocket. It did indeed reveal something bad about this guy, and I moved on.

If something happens to make you start mistrusting your doctor, talk about it openly with him. I know that's hard, but you have no choice. Remember, mistrust is a cancer that will kill your relationship if you don't heal it.

So just honestly say that you're concerned about what your doctor did. If he's defensive or dismissive, that's a bad sign. At the heart of medical training is a discussion of the mistakes student doctors make. He learned medicine by having his mistakes discussed. He should be able to handle this. If you're at all uneasy, this is definitely a time to get a second opinion.

AVOIDING CONFLICT

Here's why there can be conflict in the patient–doctor relationship. Doctors want good patients, which to them means people who are motivated to cooperate with the doctor. Patients want good doctors, which to them means doctors who treat them as equals. You see the problem. Your doctor wants a more unequal relationship than you do. It's not that he's power crazy. It's that he really does have power in the form of medical knowledge and access to medical resources. From his point of view, why should he waste time treating you like an equal when frankly you're not.

And there you are walking into his office with all kinds of material that you've printed up from websites you've visited on the Internet. You want to be taken seriously, but he doesn't want to waste his time with what feels like amateur hour.

The antidote to conflict is respect. Sometimes it's very difficult to come to agreement. But if you treat your doctor with respect, and if you insist on his treating you with respect, then there's a good chance that you'll resolve your conflict without it eating away at your relationship. And all respect means here is seeing the validity in the other person's concerns. It's valid that your doctor will be concerned with making the best use of his time. Or with using the best available medical knowledge (which isn't what you always find on the Internet). But it's valid that you'd be concerned to learn as much as possible about your illness or injury.

Here's one way to show your doctor respect that will also help him be most open minded to some alternative treatment or diagnosis you've learned about. Send your doctor the information a few days before your appointment, and attach a note saying specifically what you want your doctor to consider. This will give her time to read and think without your wasting your own appointment time. It's your best chance of getting a fair hearing.

You can make sure that you get the respect you need by asking for an explanation whenever you feel you're being opposed. For example, you can ask, "Why won't you even read this material that I brought in?" Maybe you're the tenth person that day who's brought in the same material. Maybe your doctor knows what the biases are in that material.

But if you feel that your doctor is just pulling rank on you, if the only explanation he gives amounts to "because I'm the doctor and you're just a lowly patient," then you should move on. This is not someone who's interested in working with you. He's going to make you feel frustrated and discouraged, and he's going to exacerbate your second illness.

GETTING A SECOND OPINION

The rule of thumb for when to get a second opinion couldn't be clearer: *You should feel free to get a second opinion:*

- if you've been diagnosed with something serious, or
- if the treatment prescribed is radical, expensive, or invasive, or
- or if there's a large gap between what you think should be happening in your recovery and what actually is happening.

If you want a second opinion, it's best not to go off on your own and do it behind your doctor's back, particularly if your only reason for doing this is embarrassment. Your doctor has test results, X rays, and other material that would be very useful to a doctor who's offering a second opinion.

Here's how to handle this with your doctor. Say, "because I haven't been getting better for so long [or because this is a major operation that you're recommending for me, or because your diagnosis is so serious] I think I'd like to get a second opinion." It's as simple as that. He may recommend a specialist, but he should certainly acquiesce readily.

Good doctors welcome second opinions. It's hard for lay people to understand this, because in our everyday world we'd feel insulted if someone told us that they want a second opinion when we gave them advice. But good doctors understand that a second opinion is a win/win scenario. They are getting backstopped in case the ball's gotten away from them. And if they're right, then you'll have much more confidence in what they're saying, and you'll be that much more protected against the second illness.

MAKING SURE YOUR CONCERNS ARE ADDRESSED

Almost every patient comes to her doctor with more needs than can be met in that particular visit. This isn't your doctor's fault. Time is limited and our needs are endless. So you need to help your doctor focus in on what's most important to you. That will help him do the best job, and it will help you feel satisfied with the help you're getting.

The key is your prioritizing the issues you want to deal with. A mistake people make is trying to get a few minor points out of the way before they get to the main event. I have no idea why people do this, but my patients do it with me and most doctors tell me that their patients do it with them. The list of concerns you tell your doctor about should start with the one issue you want addressed just in case nothing else gets addressed but that issue. The next issue should be the one you want to talk about if only two can be addressed. And so on.

How do you determine what this most important issue is? It's the one you think has the biggest impact on your life, or the one that makes you most afraid. It's not the most recent issue to have come up, nor is it necessarily the issue you talked about the last time you saw your doctor.

This strong focus on prioritizing may not seem like such a big deal, but it will work wonders for your sense that you're getting the most out of your relationship with your doctor. You'll certainly get the most out of your visit with your doctor.

For each issue, there are three things you need to make clear to your doctor. Say what *all* your symptoms are. Say why this is important to you. Say what you want your doctor to do about it. Sometimes all this is obvious. But lots of times it isn't, and the clearer you are about these three points, the more effective you'll feel and the more effective your doctor will be.

After getting your priorities straight, the next most important thing you can do is to bring a pad and pen to your appointment and make notes. Patients rarely remember more than one thing the doctor said to them—even really smart patients. There's too much information and too much stress for it to work out any other way. So if you want to take away all the good stuff there is to take away, you should be taking notes, just the way you did in your favorite class in school.

Those notes will feel like a godsend when you get home. You'll have information about what's wrong with you. What you can expect. What tests are required and why. What medicine is being prescribed and what side effects you have to look out for. How soon you should get better. And what exercises, dietary changes, and other self-help measures you should be taking.

16

Using Your Spirituality to Speed Your Recovery

One of the keys to healing the second illness is what I call getting ahead of the curve. You've gotten ahead of the curve when you've done everything possible to prepare for every aspect of what you're going through. And when I say everything, I mean *everything*. It could mean taking out a subscription to *Mononucleosis Monthly* if that's what you have. It could mean making an appointment to see a busy alternative healer in addition to your regular medical person. Doing online research. Talking with those closest to you about what you're going to need and how they're going to help.

And getting ahead of the curve *should* mean doing everything possible to take care of yourself from the spiritual end of things, in line with your beliefs. Of course, if you don't have any religious beliefs, that's okay. Lots of people don't.

But most people do believe in something. It could be a belief based in an organized religion or in an established spiritual practice. It could be a remnant of the religion they were brought up in. It could be a form of the New Age or Eastern spiritual beliefs that are so much in the air these days. It could just be a sense of searching based on nothing more than a conviction that there has to be "something more."

And yet many people fail to use their beliefs to help them get ahead of the curve. We get lazy. We don't know what to do. We're reluctant to take a risk. But this is an opportunity. Your illness or injury can help you to have a spiritual breakthrough that will also have a huge impact on your getting better quickly and completely.

The first thing you need to do is deepen your spirituality. Ask yourself what you believe, and what your beliefs are based on. This is your spiritual base. Now ask yourself what you can do to strengthen this base through action. Here's what I mean.

Let's say that all you really believe is that there's a God, and this is based on your experience of going to church or synagogue or mosque or temple as a kid. Well then, search for a church that's similar to the one you grew up in, one that gives you a similar kind of experience. Then just throw yourself into the religious activities there, as much as you feel comfortable with. Don't wait to "feel religious" before you start "acting religious." It doesn't work that way. If you act in ways connected to your religious or spiritual background, the feelings will follow.

But suppose you've rejected the religion of your childhood. For example, perhaps what you believe now is a more diffuse kind of spirituality, maybe somewhat Buddhist, although you're not sure, and this belief is based on a couple of books you've read or some people you've talked to. Well then, deepen *that*. Talk to more people. Read more books. Look for some spiritual home for your beliefs, a place to go to once or twice a week, even if at first it seems a little strange.

Or suppose you're a strong believer and you regularly go to services. You can deepen that too. There is no religious tradition out there that doesn't offer plenty of ways to increase your commitment and involvement. Let's put it this way. Even the Pope goes on retreat now and then.

It's always worthwhile to talk to a clergy person or spiritual practitioner about your desire to deepen your spirituality. Books are very worthwhile, but there's no substitute for one-on-one spiritual direction.

The next thing you need to do is focus your spirituality on giving you ways to deal with your illness or injury. From a religious point of view, you are 100 percent entitled to stand fully naked in front of God, showing forth the extent and depth of what you need. You should never be afraid to bring all your needs to God.

How to do this is a whole other question. I'll let you in on a secret. Most religions are very old. Whatever it is you need help with—recovering from your difficult operation, coping with failing eyesight, whatever—your religion or spiritual orientation has centuries of experience finding ways for you to present your need to God. For example, in my church, after the main service, people can come up to the altar rail for Holy Unction. They tell the minister who or what needs healing, and he anoints them with oil on their foreheads, places his hand on their heads, and offers a special prayer to God for help. It's hard to say how much people are helped physically, but they sure feel a lot better.

You can think of this as a kind of religious technology. Every religion has things like this, and they're designed to actually *work*, like all technology. I'm talking about things like how to pray, or what forms of worship you should participate in. Again, ask a member of the clergy or spiritual advisor for specific ways for you to deal on the spiritual level with what's happening to your body.

Don't count on miracles. Most spiritual orientations understand that both your relationship with God and your emotional state can be put at risk if you directly challenge the natural order and ask for a miracle. It rarely happens that when the doctors have given up hope, God swoops down and makes fools of them. Then what do you do when your prayers aren't answered?

Pray with your whole heart. It's not for me to say what the best kind of praying is from a theological point of view.

I'm not a member of the clergy. But I definitely can say what kind of praying gives the greatest boost psychologically and emotionally, particularly when you're dealing with an illness or injury. This is prayer that has three ingredients.

First, you're having a genuine conversation with God. The point is that whatever happens to your body, you're not alone. By talking to God about how you feel and what you need, being absolutely honest about what's in your heart and mind, by asking questions, by listening deeply all the way out into the darkness and silence we sometimes face when we try to contact God, it's possible to have a true sense of a healthful, helping relationship. And that relationship helps you feel better and get better faster.

Second, you're praying for the strength and wisdom to deal with whatever is happening in your body. This is a very positively oriented kind of prayer. Of course it's true that you feel weak and small and stupid about what's happening to you. But by filling your prayers with thoughts of the kind of strength and wisdom you'd like to have and that you're asking for, you're giving your prayers a chance to be answered and you're filling your head with positive thoughts. Two birds with one stone!

Third, you're praying for understanding. These prayers are really part of the conversation you're trying to have with God, but the focus is on understanding what you're going through, why it's happened, what it means, how you're supposed to respond to this change in your life, how your illness or injury is affecting the people closest to you. And this understanding can come to you through your prayer. It's no once-in-a-millennium miracle. It's a natural part of having a relationship with a higher power, but you have to work that relationship, ask questions, suggest possible answers, be wide open for new understanding, and listen, listen, listen.

Broaden your religion or spirituality. This is different from deepening it. Deepening implies a kind of intensification. Broadening means exploring paths close to but different from the spiritual path you're trying to deepen. Look, I'm not talking about Orthodox Jews attending Sunday morning services at Our Lady of Sorrows, or Tibetan Buddhists joining the choir at the First Calvary Baptist Church. I'm just talking about, for example, Orthodox Jews checking out Kabala or Hasidism. Or Catholics exploring Benedictine spirituality. Or Tibetan Buddhists exploring Zen or even allied Hindu traditions.

Think about it like this. These alternative traditions have evolved for a reason. They have something to offer. Why not see if they have something to offer *you* as you work at dealing with your illness or injury.

Finally, don't be reluctant to actively look for spiritual help. Many people have to overcome a natural reluctance to use their religious or spiritual resources to get ahead of the curve. Some people are embarrassed at "turning to God." Maybe they think family or friends will label them as religious nuts or as fair-weather friends who only care about their religion now that they need it. Some have been disappointed by religion in the past and they're reluctant to subject themselves to that kind of disappointment again.

I have an answer to this: A good religious or spiritual home solves all these problems.

I see something similar to this with people who go to see a therapist or a coach. They have one or two disappointments, and then they get down on the whole process. But religion or spirituality is not a home for just your soul. It's a home for *you*. That means you have to find a place that feels like home to you. Disappointments mean that you haven't found that home yet. But today we live as never before in history surrounded by a variety of places to go with our spiritual needs. Take your needs seriously. That means don't stop until you find a spiritual home where you can feel like yourself.

It's in this kind of spiritual home that you'll find a major resource for recovering faster and more fully.

Postscript

How do you tell your friends what this book is all about so you can make contagious the help and health you've picked up here? Here's how I think you can best sum it up:

1. People have to deal with all kinds of difficult emotions as a result of their illness or injury, and these emotions typically count for most of the distress we feel.
2. Doctors largely ignore people's emotions, preventing us from achieving the fullest, fastest recovery. This leads to our hunger for *personal medicine,* in which health-care providers would fully address our emotional needs as an essential part of the treatment we're getting.

3. To begin to meet this need, this book looks at all the important kinds of emotional fall-out and gives us ways to help deal with it, so we can achieve the fullest, fastest recovery possible.

Now it's up to you. You're holding in your hands some amazing tools. People just like you have gone through a lot to come up with these tools. But we know they work. I pray that you will use what you've found here to help yourself feel better fast.

Suggestions for Further Reading

Many of us are trying to find meaning in our accident or illness. If this is you, you must read Mira Kirshenbaum's *Everything Happens for a Reason: Finding the True Meaning of the Events in Our Lives* (Harmony, 2004). It will help you discover the gift or lesson or opportunity that lies at the heart of what you've been going through.

If you're looking for a fantastic read that is chock full of ideas for how to feel better overall, you can't do better than Mira Kirshenbaum's *The Emotional Energy Factor: The Secrets High-Energy People Use to Beat Emotional Fatigue* (Delta/Random House, 2004). It contains twenty-five easy-to-implement ways to feel more alive and happy and more like yourself.

An injury or illness is often a time for making decisions. There are decisions to make about your treatment, but this can also be an opportunity for thinking about other life decisions. To insure you make the best possible decision, I must recommend my own *What Do I Do Now?: Dr. Foster's 30 Laws of Great Decision Making* (Simon & Schuster, 2001).

If you are looking for research-based, fad-free advice on nutrition to help you feel better faster, I recommend *Eat, Drink, and Be Healthy: The Harvard Medical School Guide to Healthy Eating,* by Walter C. Willett, M.D. (Free Press, 2002); *Prevention Magazine's Nutrition Advisor: The Ultimate Guide to the Health-Boosting and Health-Harming Factors in Your Diet,* by Mark Bricklin (Rodale, 1994); and *Eating Well for Optimal Health: The Essential Guide to Bringing Health and Pleasure Back to Eating,* by Andrew Weil (Quill, 2001).

If you need to get a good night's sleep, you can't do better than *Get a Good Night's Sleep,* by Katherine Albert, M.D. (Simon & Schuster, 1999).

Exercise is more important than ever when you are dealing with an illness or injury. Two comprehensive, solid, helpful guides are *Stretch and Strengthen for Rehabilitation and Development,* by Bob Anderson (Stretching, 1984), and *The American Physical Therapy Association Book of Body Maintenance and Repair,* by Marilyn Moffat (Holt, 1999).

Pain and discomfort all too commonly accompany illness and injury. You can find extra help regardless of your diagnosis in *The Chronic Pain Solution: Your Personal Path to Pain Relief,* by James Dillard, M.D. (Bantam, 2003), and *The Truth about Chronic Pain: Patients and Professionals on How to Face It, Understand It, Overcome It,* by Arthur

Suggestions for Further Reading

Rosenfeld (Basic Books, 2003). These books are for everyone dealing with pain, not just people with chronic pain.

It is hard to find good books for dealing with the psychological and emotional aspects of specific diseases. Some good general books—not just for when you have a chronic illness but regardless of your diagnosis—are *The Art of Getting Well: Maximizing Health and Well-Being When You Have a Chronic Illness,* by David Spero (Hunter House, 2002), and *Sick and Tired of Feeling Sick and Tired: Living with Invisible Chronic Illness,* by Paul Donoghue (Norton, 2000).

When it comes to dealing with cancer, excellent help can be found in *Cancer: 50 Essential Things to Do,* by Greg Anderson (Plume, 1999), and *The Human Side of Cancer: Living with Hope, Coping with Uncertainty,* by Jimmie Holland, M.D.

If you're stuck in a bad mood—sad, anxious, or irritable—you can find extra help in *Thoughts and Feelings: Taking Control of Your Moods and Your Life,* by Martha Davis, Ph.D. (New Harbinger, 1998), and *Mind over Mood: Changing How You Feel by Changing the Way You Think,* by Dennis Greenberger (Guilford, 1995).

Fans of mind/body approaches will appreciate these classics: *Minding the Body, Mending the Mind,* by Joan Borysenko (Bantam, 1998), and *The Relaxation Response,* by Herbert Benson, M.D. (HarperTorch, 1976).

About the Author

Charles Foster, Ph.D., is director of The Chestnut Hill Institute in Boston, Massachusetts. He's been a clinician, consultant, and researcher for over twenty-five years. Dr. Foster is the author, co-author, or researcher for eleven books, some of which have gone on to win awards and become bestsellers. His books are available in over fifteen languages. Dr. Foster has advanced degrees from Brandeis University, Boston College, and the University of London, and he has lectured at Harvard Medical School. Some of his research has been conducted under grants from the National Institute of Mental Health. Dr. Foster has appeared as featured expert on a number of television shows, including the *Oprah Winfrey Show* and an ABC News *20/20* primetime special with John Stossel. The father of two grown daughters, Dr. Foster is still married to his college sweetheart. He is an avid squash and tennis player. And Dr. Foster is a member of the Parish of the Good Shepherd Episcopal Church.

Index